"The very concept of leadership implies the proposition that individuals can make a difference. This proposition has never been universally accepted."

—Arthur M. Schlesinger, Jr.

Challenges
for
School Leaders

American Association of School Administrators

1801 North Moore Street • Arlington, Virginia   22209-9988 • 703/528-0700

Other Related AASA Publications

Skills for Successful School Leaders
Profiling Excellence in America's Schools
Excellence in Our Schools: Making It Happen
Planning for Tomorrow's Schools
Bill Cook's Strategic Planning for America's Schools (videotapes and books)
Schools of the Future
A Message on Managing Change
The Role of the Principal in Effective Schools (Critical Issues Report)
Principles of Effective School District Governance and Administration
Home ● School ● Community Involvement
Partnerships: Connecting Schools and Community
Public Relations for Administrators
Business and Industry: Partners in Education
Building Morale . . . Motivating Staff (Critical Issues Report)
Teacher Incentives: A Tool for Effective Management
Some Points to Consider When You Discuss MERIT PAY
Students At Risk: Problems and Solutions (Critical Issues Report)
Effective Instructional Management
Time on Task (book and videotape)
Raising Achievement Among Minority Students

These publications and more are available from the **American Association of School Administrators** (AASA), 1801 North Moore Street, Arlington, VA 22209-9988; 703/528-0700. Price lists mailed upon request. Discounts on multiple copy orders.

Library of Congress Catalog Card Number: 88-70256

ISBN Number: 0-87652-125-1

AASA Stock Number: 021-00215

Table of Contents

FOREWORD

During the past five years, the nation's attention has again turned to American education. Books about curriculum reform even top the best-seller lists. The reports on American education have outlined a number of concerns. They have also discussed a number of possible new directions for the nation's schools.

Less publicized have been the discussions about a key element in school reform: the leaders who will be responsible for effecting changes in the schools. Yet many of the reform reports have included important recommendations about school leadership in a time of educational change.

At the same time, many business and management experts have also studied leadership from the perspective of the changing American economy. While looking at what works . . . and what doesn't . . . in American business, many of these studies have developed specific recommendations for leadership that can be applied equally well to American education as to American corporations.

Challenges for School Leaders is a compilation of the recommendations on leadership contained in the education reports and those management studies. It also outlines a number of specific issues that are identified in the education reports and shows how educational leadership might address these concerns.

In preparing this book, the American Association of School Administrators asked a representative sampling of its members to respond to a survey discussing their own concerns about leadership. The respondents were also asked to report on specific programs their schools have instituted to deal with the concerns outlined in the major education studies. The exemplary programs reported in the surveys are included throughout the book in sections titled "Promising Practices."

Each chapter concludes with a section called "Leadership in Action." These questions offer school leaders a place to start—a jumping off point for beginning discussions of educational change in local schools or school districts.

Richard D. Miller
Executive Director
American Association of School Administrators

Education Reports Addressed in This Book

A Nation At Risk. Published in 1983 by the U.S. Education Department, this report focuses primarily on the importance of curriculum reform. The report's recommendations fall into five categories: content, standards and expectations, time, teaching, and leadership and fiscal responsibilities.

A Nation Prepared: Teachers for the 21st Century. Published by the Carnegie Forum on Education and the Economy, this report examines teaching as a profession. It outlines what is necessary for what the report calls a "second wave" of reform focusing on changing the conditions of teaching in U.S. schools.

A Place Called School. This report, published by McGraw-Hill in 1983, is a condensation of the recommendations in John Goodlad's multi-year "Study of Schooling." Goodlad's work, based on visits to more than 1,000 classrooms throughout the country, recommends major changes in American schooling, including earlier starting and ending ages.

Academic Preparation for College. Published by the College Board, this multi-volume report is subtitled "What Students Need to Know and Be Able to Do." The first volume outlines a number of specific curricular recommendations for seven competencies required by all college-bound students. Companion volumes outline specific curricular recommendations in the following fields: English, the arts, mathematics, science, social studies, and foreign language.

Educating Americans for the 21st Century. This report, prepared by the National Science Foundation, focuses particularly on the importance of mathematics and science education in American schools.

High School. Written by Ernest Boyer, president of the Carnegie Foundation for the Advancement of Teaching and former U.S. Commissioner of Education, this study takes a closer look at the curriculum, staffing, and leadership necessary to change American high schools.

Horace's Compromise. This book, written by Theodore Sizer, former dean of the Harvard Graduate School of Education, reflects the results of the multi-year "Study of High Schools." Sizer proposes a major restructuring of high schools and high school curricula.

Investing in Our Children. Published by the Committee for Economic Development, whose members include 200 chief executives of businesses and universities, this report offers another perspective on school improvement and the stake that all sectors of American society have in it.

Leaders for America's Schools. This report by the National Commission on Excellence in Education focuses on leadership and the important role of educational leaders in American schools.

Time for Results: The Governors' 1991 Report on Education. This 1986 report by the National Governors' Association focuses on a number of key issues in education, including curriculum, teaching, and school facilities. It also includes a chapter on the importance of educational leadership.

Business Texts Consulted

In Search of Excellence, Thomas J. Peters and Robert H. Waterman. This best-selling 1982 book was one of the first to explore the conditions that foster excellence in American companies.

The Effective Executive. In this 1967 book, Peter Drucker, the dean of American management consultants, outlined many of the theories on management later popularized by Peters and Waterman.

Innovation and Entrepreneurship. Peter Drucker's 1985 study focuses on management practices that are part of what he calls the "discipline of innovation."

Leadership Papers. John Gardner, who has years of experience serving at the highest levels in education and government, has written five papers on various aspects of leadership: the nature of leadership, the tasks of leadership, leader-constituent interaction, leadership and power, and moral aspects of leadership.

Leadership. This 1978 book by James MacGregor Burns outlines the theory of "transforming leadership."

Thriving on Chaos. Tom Peters' 1987 book, subtitled "A Handbook for Management Revolution," outlines specific skills and strategies for managers interested in institutionalizing change.

Chapter 1

What Is Leadership?

"Managing is getting paid for home runs someone else hits."
—Casey Stengel
Former manager, New York Yankees

I n the past several years, a number of management experts have examined the qualities and characteristics of leadership. In particular, these writers have tried to examine what makes one individual an effective leader.

Most of these experts agree that there is no single model for effective leadership. Leaders have styles that range from flamboyant to self-effacing, from coldly analytical to boldly visionary. Martin Luther King, Jr., Lee Iacocca, Casey Stengel, and Dwight Eisenhower could hardly be more different in style. Yet each was an effective leader.

An excellent analysis of leadership is a series of papers written by John Gardner, former Secretary of Health, Education and Welfare and director of the Leadership Studies Program sponsored by Independent Sector, a national nonprofit coalition. In "The Nature of Leadership," Gardner identifies six special characteristics of leaders. They:

- **Think longer term**—beyond the day's crises, beyond the quarterly report, beyond the horizon.

- **Look beyond the unit they are heading** and grasp its relationship to larger realities—the larger organization of which they are a part, conditions external to the organization, global trends.

- **Put heavy emphasis on the intangibles** of vision, values, and motivation; and understand intuitively the non-rational and unconscious elements in the leader-constituent interaction.

- **Are outstanding managers** with the ability to set priorities.

- **Have the communications and political skills** to cope with the conflicting requirements of multiple constituencies.

- **Think in terms of renewal** for the organization and its people.

This chapter outlines each of these six characteristics of leadership in the context of what those *outside* education have said might bear on the task of an educational leader. The next chapter takes these same characteristics and examines them specifically within the context of educational leadership.

Long-term thinking

"The truly important events on the outside are not the trends," says noted management consultant and *Wall Street Journal* columnist Peter Drucker. "They are the changes in the trends." The ability to perceive those trends . . . and to react to them . . . is one of the characteristics that sets a leader apart. Yet far too many managers succumb to a desire to achieve short-term results . . . and an over-reliance on "what the data can support," Drucker believes.

William Agee, former chairman of Bendix, agrees that the emphasis on the short-term is a problem for many American institutions. "One of the problems in the United States, with government and business, is the very short-term, expedient approach to problems—this quarter's earnings, this year's budget: Get me through the next election or the next board meeting.'"

A dramatic example of the failure of this kind of short-term thinking was the disastrous product introduction of Coca Cola's New Coke. All the market testing that could have been done for a new product was done. But apparently no one stopped to ask the basic question, "If it ain't broke, do we need to fix it?" Consumer reaction gave the answer. Within days, Coca Cola was forced to reissue the original flavor.

The key to remaining on top, most management experts agree, is to think in the long-term. In a constantly changing world, said John Naisbitt in *Megatrends*, it is not enough simply to develop strategic plans. "Strategic planning is worthless—unless there first is a strategic vision."

Implementing the long-term vision

Earl Weaver, long-time manager of the Baltimore Orioles, was once asked why he didn't make a particular substitution that might have helped his team in the short term, but could have been damaging over the longer term. Weaver's salty explanation: "This ain't a football game. We do this every day."

Leaders share Weaver's vision. They rarely think about a single quarter or a single year. They look ahead to the "championship."

One way excellent companies express their commitment to long-term success is through their almost fanatical dedication to providing excellent service, observe Tom Peters and Robert Waterman in their influential book *In Search of Excellence*. They cite the example of Frito-Lay, which has made a commitment to a "99.5 percent service level" a major goal of the company. What does that mean in practical terms? "It means that Frito will do some things that in the short run clearly are uneconomic," Peters and Waterman note. They will, for example, spend several hundred dollars sending a truck to restock a store with $30 worth of potato chips. In the short run, such actions are no way to make money. But in the long haul, this commitment produces results . . . and profits.

How do companies attain that long-term service orientation? A Citibank survey of 18 outstanding companies found that one key element was a **"service statesman"** leader who is personally committed to the importance of good service . . . and willing to back up subordinates who will take extraordinary steps to provide it.

Experimentation and failure

A second way that leaders emphasize long-term goals rather than short-term profits is how they deal with failure. Charles Garfield suggests, "Not only do they tolerate failure, they almost seem to welcome it."

At IBM, top management quotes founder Thomas Watson: "The way to succeed is to double your failure rate." At Johnson and Johnson, leaders often quote founder General Johnson: "If I wasn't making mistakes, I wasn't making decisions." At 3M, engineers tell many stories about vice presidents who were innovators who failed repeatedly . . . until they finally achieved success.

One reason for this tolerance for failure, suggests Garfield, is that leaders are so intent on achieving their mission that the word "failure" rarely enters their conversation. Instead, he notes, they develop "scores of synonyms—glitch, bug, hitch, miss, bungle, false start . . . [to] convey their view that what someone else might call a failure is something from which they intend to learn."

Keys to Long-Term Success

- Commitment to superior service.
- Encouragement of experimentation, with a willingness to support failure.
- "Transforming" leadership.
- Teamsmanship.

Awareness of the outside

One definition of a leader is a person who sets the direction for an organization. If that definition is accurate, then it is clear that a leader must be aware of forces outside the organization. Frequently it is those forces—the economy, the nation's political mood, changing consumer behavior—that affect the outcome of an organization's activities far more than anything accomplished within the organization.

As a result, says James March in *Managing Ambiguity and Paradox*, it may be helpful to think of a new metaphor for a leader: a sailor. If one assumes that organizations are "sailed, not driven," March says, "the effectiveness of leadership often depends on being able to time small interventions so that the force of natural organizational processes amplifies the interventions rather than dampens them."

One of the dangers of new technology is that it reduces a leader's reliance on "sensing which way the wind blows" by creating the illusion that everything can be quantified. However, notes Drucker, "the relevant outside events are rarely available in quantifiable form until it is much too late to do anything about them."

And action is the key. Leaders do not succumb to "paralysis by analysis." They are not afraid to act on the information once they receive it.

An excellent historical example of this response to outside forces comes from the success of Stonewall Jackson at the Battle of Second Manassas. In the summer of 1862, two Union armies were campaigning in Virginia. General George McLellan was marching north from near Richmond and Major General John Pope was moving west from Washington. Their goal was to join forces and smash Lee's army.

Jackson, however, received word that the Union armies were on the move. He calculated where they were most likely to meet and then took a gamble, marching his men more than 50 miles in just 2 days so he could get to the meeting point first. His army's surprise attack led to a resounding defeat for the Union forces in the battle.

Vision, values, and motivation

Henry Kissinger has said that the task of a leader "is to get his people from where they are to where they have not been. . . . Leaders must invoke an alchemy of great vision."

Most students of leadership agree that the ability to articulate a vision for an organization is a key responsibility of a leader. In *Leaders*, Warren Bennis and Burt Nanus suggest that "an *essential* factor in leadership is the capacity to influence and *organize meaning* for the members of the organization."

In his book *Leadership*, James MacGregor Burns uses different words to discuss the same phenomenon. The content—paying attention to all the details, setting priorities and monitoring progress toward meeting those goals, and the other necessary activities that take up a majority of any administrator's day—Burns calls "transactional leadership."

Transforming leadership

But there is a second important type of leadership, which Burns calls "transforming leadership." It occurs, he says, "when persons with certain motives and purposes mobilize, in competition or conflict with others, institutional, political, psychological and other resources so as to arouse, engage, and satisfy the motives of followers."

Ultimately, Burns notes, there is a moral component to transforming leadership. It occurs:

> when one or more persons engage with others in such a way that leaders and followers raise one another to higher levels of motivation and morality. Their purposes, which might have started out separate but related, in the case of transactional leadership, become fused. Power bases are linked not as counterweights but as mutual support for common purpose. Various names are used for such leadership: elevating, mobilizing, inspiring, exalting, uplifting, exhorting, evangelizing. The relationship can be moralistic, of course. But transforming leadership ultimately becomes *moral* in that it raises the level of human conduct and ethical aspirations of both the leader and the led, and thus has a transforming effect on both.

Burns's theory of transforming leadership has been adopted by many of the other students of effective management. Gardner, for example, notes that the phrase has come to mean leadership "that goes beyond merely managing the system to helping the system achieve its next stage of evolution." As such, he believes, the idea is "well worth preserving." He cautions, however, that reliance on transforming leaders must not "set us dreaming again of leaders who will relieve us of the burden of responsibility."

Charles Garfield studied the importance of these transforming leaders in his book *Peak Performers*. Transforming leaders emphasize certain goals over and over again. And by doing so, Garfield notes, they "provide the *why* that inspires every *how*. It points the way."

Thomas Watson's "respect for the individual" at IBM became the foundation of IBM's entire corporate philosophy. The company's emphasis on setting achievable sales goals so that salespeople feel like winners instead of losers, for example, is a direct outgrowth of Watson's belief.

There is a similarity in the particular vision that seems to drive most transforming leaders. Howard Head, who founded the company that produces Head Skis and Prince tennis rackets, puts it this way: "You have to believe in the impossible." IBM's Watson expressed a similar belief: "We want to give the best customer service of any company in the world." And Charles Knight of Emerson Corporation uses virtually the same words: "Set and demand standards of excellence. Anybody who accepts mediocrity—in school, in job, in life—is a guy who compromises. And when the leader compromises, the whole damn organization compromises."

In fact, note Peters and Waterman, the best corporations share a few basic values:

- A belief in being the "best."
- A belief in the importance of the details of execution, the nuts and bolts of doing the job well.
- A belief in the importance of people as individuals.
- A belief in superior quality and service.
- A belief that most members of the organization should be innovators, and its corollary, the willingness to support failure.
- A belief in the importance of informality to enhance communication.
- Explicit belief in and recognition of the importance of economic growth and profits.

Managerial excellence

Some writers have made attempts to draw fine distinctions between "leaders" and "managers." In the process, notes John Gardner, "leaders generally end up looking like a cross between Napoleon and the Pied Piper, and managers like unimaginative clods." Yet leaders are measured by results: their ability to translate their vision of excellence into reality. As a result, with few exceptions, strong leaders are also good managers.

There are dozens of other books that explain the specific responsibilities of managers in great detail. However, there are three areas of management that involve an exercise of leadership:

- Setting priorities.
- Keeping the system functioning.
- Setting agendas and making decisions.

Setting priorities

There is never enough time to accomplish everything. There are pressures and crises in every organization. As a result, leaders have to establish clear priorities for themselves . . . and their organizations.

A second part of setting priorities, says Drucker, is setting "'posteriorities'—that is, deciding what tasks not to tackle—and sticking to the decision." If one tries to do everything, Drucker notes, nothing whatever will get done. The key to accomplishing priorities is to stick to them.

How can a leader set priorities? Drucker identifies "courage" as the most important requirement, and sets forth these general principles:

- Pick the future as against the past.
- Focus on the opportunity rather than the problem.
- Choose your own direction—rather than climb on the bandwagon.

● Aim high, aim for something that will make a difference, rather than for something that is "safe" and easy to do.

Keeping the system functioning

Finding ways to use employees' abilities is the greatest challenge of the manager today. The new role, however, was first described more than 50 years ago by Thomas Watson, founder of IBM. He said his managers' job was "to make sure workers have the tools and information they needed, and to help them when they found themselves in trouble."

One effective technique is to give employees greater control over their jobs. A number of studies have confirmed that when employees *feel* they have some control over their work lives, their *commitment* to their job is dramatically increased. As a result, they will work harder and do better. For example, people feel their chances of winning a lottery are much greater if they reach in to draw the winning ticket than if someone else does.

Garfield cites the example of Chaparral Steel, an American steel mill whose workers produce more tons of steel per employee per year than any steel mill in the world. Chaparral has achieved that success, at a time when many other American steel mills are closing, in part because it places decision-making power where it will be most effective. Garfield points out:

> Often that is not in the executive office. Foremen do all
> the hiring. Employees run the quality-control program
> and the safety program. Workers make decisions daily on
> the mill floor. With four levels of management, . . . work-
> ers can talk to a supervisor or the man at the top with al-
> most equal ease. As one mill hand . . . explains: "If you
> have a good idea, somebody's gonna listen to you and
> that tends to make you think a little harder, go a little fur-
> ther out of your way, do things a little better.

Setting agendas and making decisions

There are, Gardner notes, leaders who can motivate and inspire, but who cannot translate that motivation into a course of action that will bring lasting results. Yet the ultimate test of a leader is whether he or she has brought about lasting change.

John F. Kennedy had the ability to set agendas. When he announced the goal of putting a man on the moon before 1970, he galvanized an entire nation. Congress appropriated funds. NASA hired the best scientists. And the seemingly impossible was accomplished. Yet, noted John Naisbitt, that agenda was successful precisely because it was specific. If Kennedy had said, "We are going to be the world leader in space exploration," Naisbitt notes, there would have been no such organizing focus—and it is possible the goal would not have been achieved.

Communications/political skills

The best leaders are outstanding communicators. They have the ability to inspire others to join in their vision of the future, and to commit themselves to the overall goal of the organization. Today, the number of groups with whom a leader is expected to communicate has increased dramatically.

For example, when Lee Iacocca became president of Chrysler Corporation, his official "constituency" was the Chrysler shareholders. But to accomplish the job of making the company profitable again, he needed to deal with a number of other constituencies—labor leaders, government representatives, the press, suppliers, bankers, employees, and other members of the management team.

And that very act of communication, says management consultant Tom Peters in *Thriving on Chaos*, makes a leader "political, in the very best and purest sense of that word. He or she . . . is constantly out 'campaigning'—campaigning for the support, energy, and whole-hearted participation of everyone in the organization."

The stump speech

One technique some leaders have borrowed from politicians is to develop a "stump speech"—a three- to five-minute talk that emphasizes the basic themes of a campaign. The speech, with variations, can be used in both formal and informal meetings to motivate listeners to share, and act on, the leader's vision.

In today's pluralistic society, most leaders have *many* constituencies, not just one. And trying to develop a position that makes all the constituency groups happy can be an impossible task. As a result, Gardner says, leaders "must consider the needs of their multiple constituencies, the demands of powerful interest groups and finally, one hopes, their own best judgment."

Renewal

The ultimate task of a leader, Gardner says, is to help the organization renew itself. Because external conditions are constantly changing, organizations need to change in response to those conditions. Yet any renewal, Gardner says, should be directed toward "the kind of change that will preserve our deepest values, enhance the vitality of the system, and ensure its future."

The belief in renewal keeps organizations dynamic. It prevents people from succumbing to the fallacy that, "There will always be a need for a well-run buggy whip factory," say Peters and Waterman. And, notes Burns in *Leadership*, there is another significant benefit to renewal:

> Transforming leadership is dynamic leadership in the
> sense that the leaders throw themselves into a relation-
> ship with followers who will feel "elevated" by it and
> often become more active themselves, thereby creating
> new cadres of leaders.

One way that leaders accomplish the goal of ensuring organizational renewal is by making as few decisions as possible. They assemble the strongest possible team . . . and then let those people make decisions. As Peter
Drucker has commented:

> There is no prouder boast, but also no better prescrip-
> tion, for executive effectiveness than the words Andrew
> Carnegie, the father of the U.S. steel industry, chose for
> his own tombstone: "Here lies a man who knew how to
> bring into his service men better than he was himself."

Team leadership

Gardner concurs, pointing out that most effective leadership "involves
a number of individuals acting in a team relationship." Assembling this team
is important because the tasks of leadership today are so complex that almost no one can be expected to be outstanding in all of them. Corporate
boards, Gardner notes, frequently understand this better than other organizations. If they select an outstanding speaker and motivational visionary
person as CEO, the board will frequently appoint a deputy who has strong-
er skills in management and finance, for example. "The important thing is
not that the leader cover all bases, but that the team collectively does so,"
Gardner concludes.

There is a real similarity between the recommendations of the management experts and some of the most important education reports. The next
chapter looks at those similarities, and also discusses specific recommendations about leadership taken from the education reports.

What Education Reports Say About Leadership

"Strong leaders create strong schools. Research and common sense suggest that administrators can do a great deal to advance school reform. I believe that they must and will lead the second wave of reform."

—Bill Clinton
Governor of Arkansas

Each of the six key responsibilities of leadership identified by John Gardner is also identified in the important education reports. This chapter discusses some of the recommendations of those reports in the context of Gardner's key responsibilities.

Many of the education reports specifically discuss the importance of leadership. In *High School,* for example, Boyer notes, "If the goals we set forth in this report are to be accomplished, strong leadership will be needed to pull together the separate elements in the school and make them work."

School administrators, too, recognize the importance of leadership in their jobs. Researcher Susan Krouner Sclafani conducted a study for the University of Texas to determine whether the performance goal areas and skills identified by the American Association of School Administrators (AASA) as guidelines for the preparation of school administrators are in fact perceived by superintendents as most important to effective performance in the superintendency. Superintendents who were interviewed for the research project were asked to rank 52 skills in their order of importance. Respondents indicated that "using a broad array of leadership skills" is most important for effective performance as a superintendent.

Long-term thinking

In *The Lessons of History,* Will and Ariel Durant observed, "The future never just happened. It was created."

Several of the major education reports have taken a look at the future of education. They have noted that in the next 10 to 20 years, a number of major changes will dramatically affect the schools. These include changing student populations, changing teacher demographics, and a changing economy.

The National Governors' Association (NGA) report, *Time for Results: The Governors' 1991 Report on Education,* examines many of these changes. The governors agreed that "school leadership will be a key ingredient" in planning for the future. Specifically, the NGA report noted the need for an "integrated approach" to planning.

Theodore Sizer agrees. In *Horace's Compromise,* he notes, "Late-twentieth century high schools deserve a more appropriate purpose than a warmed-over version of principles promulgated in 1918."

Many of the major reports have offered specific suggestions. Mortimer Adler's *Paideia Proposal,* for example, creates a distinction among three spheres of learning: the development of intellectual skills, the acquisition of knowledge, and the enlargement of understanding of ideas and values. He suggests that school leaders reexamine the structure of schools and the content of the curriculum with these three spheres of learning in mind.

John Goodlad offers another approach. In *A Study of Schooling,* he proposes what he calls "rethinking the continuum of schooling"—with children beginning school at age 4 and completing secondary education by age 16.

Sizer also calls for a basic rethinking of the structure of secondary education:

> The school's goals should be simple: that each student
> master a limited number of centrally important skills and
> areas of knowledge. While these skills and areas will, to
> varying degrees, reflect the traditional academic disci-
> plines, the program's design should be shaped by the in-
> tellectual and imaginative powers and competencies that
> students need, rather than by "subjects" as conven-
> tionally defined.

Many of these specific recommendations are discussed in greater detail in Chapter 5 of this book. However, even this brief discussion makes it clear that some of the most significant recommendations of the education reports are calling on school leaders to begin a substantial reexamination of schooling and a reevaluation of educational priorities.

School leaders need to devote time to other kinds of long-range planning, as well. The NGA report cited a 1984 survey by the National School

Boards Association, which found that although 96 percent of school districts were using computers for instructional purposes, only 14 percent had planned how they were going to purchase and use software.

Long-range planning is a key function—perhaps the most important function—of educational leaders. Yet the job of school administrator as it is currently structured frequently makes long-term planning difficult . . . if not virtually impossible. Research shows that a typical principal's day, for example, consists of more than 150 *separate* interactions, most of them brief, and virtually all of them dealing with specific, concrete, and pressing problems. This kind of fragmented day leaves little time for long-term planning.

Unfortunately, many of the recommendations designed to help business executives find time for long-range planning are not appropriate for school leaders. Several management experts recommend, for example, that an executive set aside certain times during each day for quiet work and reflection. This is difficult, to say the least, in the very active setting of a school office.

Some promising alternatives might include:

- Periodically freeing school administrators from their day-to-day responsibilities so they can visit other schools, attend conferences or workshops, or engage in other planning.
- Devoting concentrated time to long-range planning during the summer months.
- Adopting a program of shared decision making, as outlined in Chapter 3.

One final avenue to facilitate long-range planning is for school districts to adopt a recommendation included in the NGA report and create a districtwide panel to review the national education reports. The panel, which might include parents, education leaders, business leaders, and other concerned citizens, could consider the following questions:

- What do the education reports recommend?
- Are these recommendations the right agenda for our district?
- What facts do we have to help us outline our district's agenda?
- What will it take for us to succeed?
- What resources do we have that we can build on?
- How will we know we have reached our goal?

Awareness of the outside

Many of the most dramatic changes in education are the result of changes that are outside the influence of school administrators. The major education reports discuss a number of these changes. They include:

Teachers

In *A Nation Prepared: Teachers for the 21st Century,* the Carnegie Forum predicts that the nation may need more than one million new teachers in the next five years. Chapter 4 discusses this prediction and analyzes a number of other major education reports on teaching. In the face of such a shortage, school leaders will need to develop creative new approaches for attracting, motivating, and rewarding teachers.

Changing students and families

Demographic changes have produced a student population with significantly more students who are deemed at risk. In *A Nation Prepared,* the Carnegie Forum noted:

> As the world economy changes shape, it would be fatal to assume that America can succeed if only a portion of our school children succeed. By the year 2000, one out of every three Americans will be a member of a minority group. At present, one out of four American children is born into poverty, and the rate is increasing. While it was once possible for people to succeed in this society if they were simply willing to work hard, it is increasingly difficult for the poorly educated to find jobs. A growing number of permanently unemployed people seriously strains our social fabric.

The report summarized the problem by noting that it "rejects the view that America must choose between quality and equity in education policy. It cannot afford to do so."

Chapter 6 discusses the changing student population and outlines some of the programs, curricula, and instructional approaches that school leaders may wish to consider as they plan to meet this need.

Technology

The NGA report notes that "technologies available to schools are changing rapidly. New versions of computers, videotape players, satellite transmission equipment, digital television, and materials to use with technologies are produced literally every month."

These technologies, says the Carnegie Forum, "have a very limited capacity as teachers, but they can make possible student gains in crucial areas of the curriculum that might be very difficult to achieve otherwise." Schools across the country are using computers to improve student writing, notate students' musical scores, and help students learn basic engineering principles as they design and build computer-controlled experiments. In all these cases, students are using the computer as a *tool* to accomplish these tasks.

The coming "information economy" will require students to develop different skills than they have in the past, and will require school leaders to look at curriculum in a new way. Chapter 7 describes one innovative partnership that is pointing the way to the classroom of the future.

An awareness of these outside forces can help school leaders in three important ways:

- First, it can be used to develop long-range plans to address these important issues.
- Second, knowledge of the world outside an individual school or district can be useful in adapting or adopting programs that have been successful elsewhere.
- Finally, it can help school administrators develop and articulate their own long-term vision.

Vision, values, and motivation

The National Governors Association (NGA) reviewed extensive research about what makes an effective educational leader. The first requirement, they found, was that effective leaders have "clear, informed visions of what they wanted their schools to become."

Other educational researchers agree. Researcher Thomas Sergiovanni has conducted a number of studies to determine the factors that are responsible for excellence in education. His studies have led him to a belief that a vision, a sense of mission, and a commitment to excellence are what make a school excellent instead of merely acceptable.

John E. Roueche and George A. Baker studied a number of schools that had received 1983 Excellent School Awards issued by the U.S. Department of Education and published their findings in *Profiling Excellence in America's Schools*. They found that the school administrator who "defines, strengthens, and articulates purposes, beliefs, and values becomes a cultural leader capable of inspiring the best in everyone."

Father Theodore Hesburgh, former president of Notre Dame, exercised leadership in both education and civil rights. He once observed that "the very essence of leadership is [that] you have to have a vision. It's got to be a vision you articulate clearly and forcefully on every occasion. You can't blow an uncertain trumpet."

Managerial excellence

Most school administrators are excellent managers. Many, however, are frustrated by the amount of time they must spend on management. *High School* quoted one principal:

> When I started as a principal, the assistant superintendent advised me, 'Harold, 75 percent of your time should

be spent in evaluation, instruction, and curriculum.' I
couldn't even do it then. Today, it's reversed. I don't
spend 25 percent of my time with the people who are
handling the instructional program!

One of the greatest challenges for educational leaders in the future,
however, will be developing skills of managing for change. As schools engage in a process of self-renewal, educational leaders will have to serve as
change agents.

One possible solution, suggested in both *Horace's Compromise* and *A
Nation Prepared*, might be to create ways for teachers and principals to in-
novate. Ask a school what it might take for that school to raise its academic
achievement by a measurable degree. Meet with every part of the school
community—teachers, students, administrators, parents, other staff members—and ask them to identify *opportunities* and *obstacles*. Work toward
removing as many of the obstacles to their performance as possible. Provide
them with as much support—financial, personal, and political—as possible.
And then let everyone in the district know of the results.

Communication/political skills

One of the keys to effecting educational change is building the necessary support for change. Support must come from both *inside* schools—
from teachers and staff—and from the *outside* community as well.

A Nation At Risk, for example, says, "Principals and superintendents
must play a crucial leadership role in developing school and community
support for the reforms we propose." The report goes on to identify three
keys to building this support:
● Persuasion.
● Setting goals.
● Developing community consensus.
John Goodlad goes even further in arguing the importance of communication:

If it is a message that educators and others are looking
for, let that message be couched in the most compelling
terms and have the highest professional appeal. The time
has come, past come, for the 50 states to articulate as
basic policy a commitment to a broad array of educational goals . . . that have emerged in this country over more
than 300 years.

Of course, as George Bernard Shaw once noted, "The greatest problem
of communication is the illusion that it has been accomplished." The AASA
publication *Building Public Confidence in Our Schools* outlines a number

of key questions to ask when developing a communications plan:

- If we're going to be successful in our school system, our school or in this school program, *who* needs to know, be involved or understand? Whose advice do we need? Who will be affected?
- If we are going to be successful, *what* do each of these groups need to understand?
- What communications channels or activities will we use to get the message through or to involve people in the process?

Renewal

Most of the education reports focus on the key role of the principal in bringing about needed reforms. John Goodlad, who studied more than 1,000 classrooms in writing *A Place Called School* (and its companion book, *A Study of Schooling*), noted:

> Schools will improve slowly, if at all, if reforms are thrust upon them. Rather, the approach having most promise, in my judgment, is one that will seek to cultivate the capacity of schools to deal with their own problems, to become largely self-renewing.

Given that vital importance, one might expect that most districts would devote considerable time and energy to selecting and training the best people for the job. In fact, following Drucker's advice to "build on strengths," the responsibility of developing the next generation of educational leaders might be seen as a vital responsibility of school leaders. That is exactly what Goodlad proposes:

> I recommend that each district superintendent take as first order of business responsibility for selecting promising prospective principals and developing in them—and in present principals—the ability to lead and manage. In fulfilling this role, it may be necessary for the superintendent to lead and manage.

Certainly that is true in the business world. Major corporations typically make managers responsible for identifying and grooming potential successors. Alfred Sloan, founder of General Motors, said he spent more time on personnel decisions than on any other aspect of management.

In practice, the selection of principals turns out to be quite different. Boyer calls the process "strikingly quixotic." The process almost amounts to self-selection—those individuals who decide to pursue advanced degrees in education or educational administration may not always be those that the district feels are most capable. And, NGA points out, school districts typically spend about one-tenth of what private industry devotes to training and developing personnel.

AASA noted in "Guidelines for the Preparation of School Administrators" that if selection and training of administrators is not improved, it will "soon translate into burdens to be endured by generations of adults."

How can current school leaders address the problems of renewing the profession? One way is to establish districtwide policies that will make sure the most qualified people become school administrators. John Goodlad outlined a two-part program:

- Establish districtwide programs to identify promising candidates for leadership. "There should be a continuous districtwide effort to identify employees with leadership potential," Goodlad notes. One clue to this potential, he suggests, is recognition by peers.

- Second, invest in the future of the district by grooming potential candidates for the principalship. "Once identified as promising, potential candidates should be added to a list of persons scheduled for paid two-year study leaves, to be taken at a major university offering a carefully planned program," Goodlad suggests. "There always should be candidates available for each vacated principalship who have been groomed for the post."

Goodlad also suggests that schools should select "from a pool of qualified applicants extending far beyond district lines." The NGA report goes even farther, recommending that states develop alternative certification mechanisms "so that candidates who have distinguished themselves as leaders in the public and private sector" could become principals.

Many current school administrators feel that their own professional preparation was inadequate. *High School* cited a survey of more than 500 districts which found that administrators frequently gave their own college and university training low marks. To provide this needed professional development, assessment centers, such as AASA's National Executive Development Center (NEDC), will be a valuable tool. In developing the center, AASA worked with the University of Texas in identifying skills of outstanding school administrators. The skills identified include:

- Leadership.
- Personnel management.
- Financial and cash flow management.
- School/community public relations and coalition building.
- Evaluation of teacher performance.
- Sound and cost-effective budgeting.
- Motivational techniques.
- Conflict mediation and coping with controversy.
- Valid and reliable performance measures for instructional outcomes.
- Sound curriculum design and instructional delivery systems.
- Human relations skills.

Through the NEDC, practicing school administrators will be able to assess their own administrative skills and then participate in a broad-based program of professional growth and development.

The next chapter takes a closer look at one of the important recommendations shared by both education reports and business experts: the importance of sharing decision making.

Chapter 3

Sharing Decision Making

> *"Rebuilding excellence in education means reaffirming
> the importance of the local school and freeing
> leadership to lead."*
>
> —Ernest Boyer
> Former U.S. Commissioner of Education

Most of the major education reports have reached the conclusion that schools must work harder at sharing the authority for making important decisions. Here are some excerpts:

- "Greater trust [must] be placed on the individual schools. Teachers and administrators should have increased decision-making power." *(Investing in Our Children)*
- "If teachers are given autonomy and held ultimately accountable for the work of their students . . . they will perform to the best of their imaginative ability. Equally important, the career of teacher will become more attractive than it is now. Talented people seek jobs that entrust them with important things." *(Horace's Compromise)*
- "Testimony before the commission, the large body of research on effective schools, and the emerging wisdom from business management all indicate that teachers should participate in the management of schools. . . . Decisions should be made closer to the classroom." *(Time for Results)*
- "If the role of the principal is to be strengthened, more authority must be given to the local school." *(High School)*
- "Professional autonomy is the first requirement. If the schools are to compete successfully with medicine, architecture, and accounting for staff, then teachers will have to have comparable authority in making the key decisions about the services they render. Within the context of a limited set of clear goals for students set by state and local policy makers, teachers, working together, must be free to exercise their professional judgment as to the best way to achieve these goals. This means the ability to make—or at least to strongly influence—decisions concerning such things as the materials and instructional methods to

be used, the staffing structure to be employed, the organization of the school day, the assignment of students, the consultants to be used, and the allocation of resources available to the school." *(A Nation Prepared)*

● "There should be . . . some kind of policy and planning group chaired by the principal and including teachers, students, parents, perhaps a nonparent, and, if possible, a representative from the district office. . . . This body would be constantly alert to problems affecting the school as a whole, would identify the need for new policies, and would be responsible for final approval of the planning document and budget prepared for discussion by the principal with the superintendent." *(A Place Called School)*

What business literature has to say about decentralization

Most of the business literature also includes recommendations for decentralizing authority for making decisions:

● "Effective executives do not make a great many decisions. They concentrate on the important ones. They try to think through what is strategic and generic, rather than solve problems. They try to make the few important decisions on the highest level of conceptual understanding." (Peter Drucker, *The Effective Executive*)

● "One reason why the Roman Empire grew so large and survived so long—a prodigious feat of management—is that there was no railway, car, airplane, radio, paper, or telephone. Above all, no telephone. And therefore you could not maintain any illusion of direct control over a general or provincial governor; you could not feel at the back of your mind that you could ring him up, or he could ring you, if a situation cropped up which was too much for him, or that you could fly over and sort things out if they started to get into a mess. You appointed him, you watched his chariot and baggage train disappear over the hill in a cloud of dust and that was that. . . . There was, therefore, no question of appointing a man who was not fully trained, or not quite up to the job: You knew that everything depended on his being the best man for the job before he set off. And so you took great care in selecting him; but more than that, you made sure that he knew all about Rome and Roman government and the Roman army before he went out." (Anthony Jay, *Management and Machiavelli: An Inquiry into the Politics of Corporate Life*)

How can schools decentralize?

The consensus of opinion from a number of the major education reports is that schools must begin to decentralize decision making. Ironically, these recommendations come at a time when more and more decisions are being made at the state level. They also come at a time when school systems are larger and more complex than ever. The nation's largest school system, in New York City, today enrolls as many children as there were people of all ages in Massachusetts during the time of Horace Mann . . . and as many as there were in all the nation's secondary schools in 1911.

Nonetheless, even the NGA report strongly urges states to give greater autonomy to local districts, districts to give more authority to local schools, and schools to give more autonomy to teachers.

Management experts note several benefits to this shared decision making:

- It benefits *teachers* by developing greater motivation for their work.
- It benefits *principals* by giving them more time to concentrate on their key priority: instructional leadership.
- It benefits *superintendents* by allowing them to concentrate on long-range planning and communicating that vision to everyone inside and outside the schools who can help make it a reality.
- It benefits *students* by providing them the education that is most likely to meet their needs.

Benefits to teachers

Providing teachers with increased involvement in decision making will help meet one of the most important conditions for improving the status and quality of the teaching force in the 1990s and beyond. The challenge, say the Carnegie Forum report and a number of other significant education reports, is to upgrade the professionalism of the teaching profession. *A Nation Prepared* notes:

> Organizations that employ professionals are . . . typically based on collegial relationships among the professionals, [although] that does not mean no one is in charge. . . . Work in such organizations is often challenging and fulfilling. A large body of research shows that it is these conditions of work, at least as much as the high salaries that typically accompany [them], that attract our most able college graduates.

And Sara Lightfoot, Harvard education professor, concurs. "Unless there are some freedoms within teaching," she says, "you will attract not creative, bright, and energetic people but more passive types who depend on bureaucracy to provide a lifetime of relatively low-risk work."

What decisions should teachers make? Many experts agree that teachers can and should be the primary decision makers about classroom instruction. For example, in *A Place Called School,* John Goodlad suggests:

> [Teachers] should have some funds to spend as they see
> fit. It should be acceptable, for instance, for a teacher to
> request and obtain 6 copies of each of 5 books rather
> than 30 of a single book for a particular class, if the re-
> quest were subjected to appropriate internal review. This
> type of ordering usually is more expensive but frequently
> is more cost-effective.

The NGA report identifies a number of other areas in which teachers
might be involved in making decisions:
- Discipline.
- School goals.
- Teachers' continuing education.
- Curriculum.
- Schoolwide problem solving.

Of course, the reports note that such increased authority carries with
it significant new responsibilities as well. The Carnegie Forum, for example,
notes that school districts "will have to develop means to assure themselves
that students are making satisfactory progress toward agreed upon goals."
The report also emphasizes that "teachers have to be prepared to accept a
greater degree of accountability in return for increased discretion."

There are a number of school districts that regularly involve teachers
in making substantive decisions about such important topics as curriculum
development, supervising new teachers, and providing inservice training.
Chapter 4 describes some of these successful programs.

Benefits to principals

The job of the principal will undergo the most dramatic change if rec-
ommendations like those made by the Carnegie Forum, NGA, and Boyer are
implemented. At the same time, many of the decisions principals now make
might become the responsibility of teachers. Specifically, both *A Nation
Prepared* and *A Place Called School* have identified decisions that could re-
ceive more attention at the school level:
- Establishing budget priorities.
- Determining staffing patterns.
- Selecting curriculum and instructional materials.
- Determining the best use of instructional space.

John Goodlad describes the new responsibilities of school principals:

> What I am proposing is genuine decentralization of au-
> thority and responsibility to the local school within a
> framework designed to assure school-to-school equity
> and a measure of accountability. Each school is to be
> held responsible for providing a balanced program of
> studies. Each school is to develop and present its pro-

gram and accompanying planning document to the superintendent through the principal.

These changes would benefit principals by freeing them up to make
important decisions affecting their school. It would, as some theorists have
described it, give principals more time for doing the *right things* than just
doing things right.

Benefits to superintendents

Superintendents would also benefit dramatically from the proposed
changes in decision making. They would be freed to devote considerable
time to making the truly important decisions that would affect the school
system for years to come. As Peter Drucker has noted:

> Time, in large, continuous, and uninterrupted units is
> needed for such decisions as whom to put on a task force
> set up to study a specific problem; what responsibilities
> to entrust to the manager of a new organizational unit or
> to the new manager of an old organizational unit; [whom]
> to promote into a vacancy.

For example, Goodlad suggests one way in which superintendents
could establish and reinforce district goals even under a system of decentralized management:

> The essence of the district-school relationship is the re-
> view process, in which the principal presents and justifies
> the plans developed under his leadership. The superin-
> tendent, in turn, following appropriate consultation,
> should be free to allocate discretionary funds to support
> unusually creative efforts and to deny funds for failure to
> plan.

Decentralization could give school superintendents more time to focus
on the truly system-changing decisions, while also fostering what Goodlad
calls "an increased sense of ownership on the part of those associated with
the local school." In turn, the representative school board, on behalf of the
community, needs to support the superintendent and other administrators
in their decisions. In a school system of any size, the administration needs
the latitude to make decisions within the policies of the organization.

Benefits to students

A more decentralized approach to decision making would benefit students by making their schools, in Peters' and Waterman's words, "closer to

the customer." As Sizer notes, "the energy and morale of the teachers are crucial influences on the success of the students." He continues:

> If the goals for students are clear ("These are the areas
> you need to master for your diploma") and relevant . . .
> student energy, much more often than not, will be pro-
> ductively focused.

Goodlad points out that by decentralizing authority, school districts will enable schools to better respond quickly to conditions that need changing. "If children's reading attainments appear to be declining, improved reading will become a top priority item on the school renewal agenda," he suggests.

Turning the Organization Chart Upside Down

In addition to emphasizing shared decision making, school leaders may find another technique useful in their efforts to create excellence in their schools. This technique has been identified by a number of management experts as one of the factors in creating a successful corporation. One example comes from the story of SAS Airlines.

Year after year, SAS ranks first in surveys of passenger satisfaction. At the same time, its profits have increased dramatically. SAS Chairman Jan Carlzon is most frequently credited for the success of the corporation. How did he do it? According to Naisbitt and Aburdene, Carlzon literally "turned the organization chart upside down."

In a typical organization chart, those employees who have the *greatest* contact with customers are found at the bottom of the chart. Carlzon put them at the top. He made it clear that it was the duty of everyone in the organization—CEO included—to provide the service to those who directly served the customers. And he let it be known that would be the basis on which everyone else would be evaluated.

William McGowan, who founded the long-distance telephone company MCI, also recognized the importance of changing the organization chart. His approach, however, was even more radical than Carlzon's: Whenever McGowan met with new managers, he would tell them, "I know that some of you, with your business-school backgrounds, are out there already beginning to draw up organization charts and starting to write manuals for operating procedures. As soon as I find out who you are, I'm going to fire every last one of you."

Two keys to successful decentralization

Loose-tight

Peters and Waterman looked at a number of companies in which there appeared to be little or no organization chart. Decisions were made from the bottom up rather than from the top down. Yet in many cases, these companies turned out to be the most cohesive. The reason, they found, was that excellent companies shared a sense of vision about who they were and what they were doing. At the same time, they shared a commitment to staying close to the customer, to providing the best possible service.

> A set of shared values and rules about discipline, details, and execution can provide the framework in which practical autonomy takes place routinely. . . . Too much overbearing discipline of the wrong kind will kill autonomy. But the more rigid discipline, the discipline based on a small number of shared values . . . in fact, induces practical autonomy and experimentation throughout the organization.

The NGA report adopts Peters' and Waterman's "loose/tight" terminology. It urges state and local authorities to be "explicit about expected levels of academic performance." On the other hand, the report says, "Then they should allow teachers, administrators, and parents to devise ways to meet these levels." In other words, the best leaders are *enablers*, not roadblockers.

Commitment to communication

The other key component to shared decision making is *communication*. Peters and Waterman note that communication is absolutely vital in fostering a shared decision-making process. They quote a manager at Hewlett Packard:

> We're really not sure exactly how the innovative process works. But there's one thing we do know: The easy communications, the absence of barriers to talking to one another are essential. Whatever we do, whatever structure we adopt, whatever systems we try, that's the cornerstone—we won't do anything to jeopardize it.

They outline five attributes of communication systems that seem to foster innovation:
- Communications are informal.
- Communication intensity is extraordinary.

- Communication is given physical supports—chalkboards, conference rooms, rooms for informal meetings.
- The organization seeks other ways to foster and institutionalize innovation.
- The intense, informal communication system acts as a remarkably tight control system.

Leadership in Action: Sharing Decision Making

As schools and districts begin to evaluate their decision-making processes, school leaders might consider the following questions:

- Are you making too many decisions? Are there others in your school or school system who could make some of them?

- What decisions should be the responsibility of building principals?

- What decisions should be the responsibility of teachers?

- How can you begin to change your district's decision-making process?

- How can parents and other community members assume some responsibility for decision making? On what decisions is it appropriate to involve the community?

- What would happen if you turned your school district's organizational chart upside down?

- How effective is your school of school district's communication program in fostering innovation? How can you make it more likely to foster innovation?

Attracting, Motivating, and Rewarding Good Teachers

"Next to funding and keeping good teachers, the other tasks of school reform pale."

—Council for Basic Education

ormer U.S. Commissioner of Education Ernest Boyer says that many of the education reforms instituted in the past five years "have just washed over most teachers." As a result, a number of major studies have urged a "second wave" of reforms to focus on improving teaching in American schools. Besides *High School,* the reports that focus on teaching include *A Nation Prepared,* by the Carnegie Forum; *Investing in Our Children,* by the Committee for Economic Development; *Who Will Teach Our Children,* by the California Commission on the Teaching Profession; *Tomorrow's Teachers,* by the Holmes Group; and *A Call for Change in Teacher Education,* by the American Association of Colleges for Teacher Education (AACTE). (See Figure 4-1)

These reports agree on a number of basic issues. First, in view of a possible shortage of teachers in some districts, American schools are facing an increasing need to attract qualified classroom teachers. Both the quality and the quantity of teachers in the future are major considerations. Second, school administrators and boards of education need to find ways to motivate the performance of all teachers. Third, districts need to look for new ways to reward outstanding teachers.

Across the country, many school leaders have already accepted the challenges of instituting this "second wave" of reforms. This chapter discusses the importance of attracting, motivating, and rewarding good teachers. It also outlines some of the successful programs operating in American schools.

FIGURE 4-1

What the Education Reports Say About Improving Teaching

RECOMMENDATIONS ON TEACHING	NGA	HS	CAR	PLACE	SIZER	NSB
Improve teacher compensation for beginning teachers	•	•	•	•	•	•
Improve teacher compensation throughout the teaching career	•	•	•	•	•	•
Alternative career structures— Provide increasing levels of responsibility and compensation	•	•	•	•	•	•
Redesign teacher training/connect with schools	•	•	•	•	•	•
Improve basic working conditions for teachers		•	•		•	•
Institute teacher recognition programs		•				•
Encourage more minority applicants			•			
Increase teachers' authority— curriculum		•	•	•	•	
Use partnerships to increase teacher compensation, motivate teachers		•				•

Key: National Governors Association (NGA); *High School* (HS); *Tomorrow's Teachers,* the Carnegie Forum report (CAR); *A Place Called School* (PLACE); *Horace's Compromise* (SIZER); *Educating Americans for the 21st Century* (NSB).

Attracting good teachers

Is a teacher shortage really on the horizon? Many educational experts think a shortage is likely. Among those who have expressed concern:

- The Carnegie Forum, which estimated that 1.3 million new teachers will be needed between 1986 and 1992.
- The National Governors' Association, which cited federal government estimates that by 1992, the supply of teachers will be only 64 percent of expected demand.
- The Western Interstate Commission for Higher Education (WICHE), which reports that the percentage of female college freshmen interested in teaching dropped from 37.5 percent in 1968 to 9.5 percent in 1985.
- The Metropolitan Life survey of teachers, which indicated 27 percent

of those in the classroom expect to leave teaching during the next five years.

In some schools, and in some specialized subject areas, the teacher shortage is already a reality. NGA reports that 43 states already have a shortage of qualified math teachers, and 42 states cannot find enough qualified physics teachers to fill all their vacancies. Similar shortages exist in special education, bilingual education, and some foreign languages.

A worsening problem

And the teacher shortage may get worse. The National Education Association estimates that between 30 and 50 percent of the nation's teaching force will retire between 1990 and 1995. The Carnegie Task Force predicted that some districts might have to replace half their teachers before 1990.

At the same time, schools need an increasing number of teachers. One reason is that schools are enrolling more students. The National Center for Education Statistics forecasts that between 1985 and 1993, school enrollments will rise by a total of about 2.9 million students. Some of the increase is being caused by the "baby echo"—the young adults born in the Baby Boom years who are now having families of their own. In addition, some states face enrollment increases because of the growing numbers of immigrant children who are enrolling in their schools.

Teacher shortages will also occur because of increased demand for teachers in some subject areas. New state-imposed graduation requirements in foreign language, for example, caused teacher shortages in New York state schools, the Rand Corporation found. Teachers for subjects such as bilingual education and special education are in demand in states with large populations of non-English-speaking immigrants.

Special shortages in math and science

The fields facing the most severe shortages are math and science. In part, these shortages are the result of recent increases in graduation requirements, which have increased the numbers of students enrolling in math and science courses. But the shortage also results from the increased career opportunities available to math and science majors. A smaller percentage of college math and science majors are choosing to go into teaching in the first place. And increasing numbers of math and science teachers are leaving teaching for more lucrative professions. In fact, one survey by WICHE found that math and science teachers were five times as likely to leave the schools for non-teaching jobs as teachers in other subject areas.

Because of the serious shortages of math and science teachers, the National Science Commission report found, many school systems have already "been forced to disregard state certification requirements and fill the gaps with unqualified instructors hired on an emergency basis." In fact, the National Science Teachers Association estimates today that nearly 30 percent of the nation's science and mathematics teachers are not qualified to teach those subjects.

Qualifications

Not everyone agrees that a shortage of teachers is imminent, of course. In fact, one study by education writer C. Emily Feistritzer suggests that because teaching follows the laws of supply and demand, no large-scale shortage of teachers is likely.

It is certainly true that those analyzing the teacher shortage may disagree about the precise figures. It is also true that no teacher shortages may exist in some regions of the country . . . today *or* in the future. But there is now a general consensus that the United States is facing a significant shortage of *qualified* elementary and secondary teachers.

A key word in any discussion of teacher shortages is "qualified." Some of those who argue that there is no impending large-scale shortage of teachers appear to solve the problem of teacher supply by interchanging the words "qualified" and "certified." The National Science Board responds:

> A qualified teacher is one adequately prepared to teach
> the subject. A certified teacher is one licensed to teach
> the subject, even if unqualified and licensed on an emer-
> gency basis.

Some graduates—even graduates of excellent programs—may have received an excellent undergraduate education, but "in fact have little knowledge of the key material taught in high schools," says Theodore Sizer in *Horace's Compromise.* For example, he says, history majors may have good training in history, but no real exposure to other social sciences that are important in teaching social studies. English majors "may be exhaustively prepared as literary critics, but know nothing of the systematic craft of writing or linguistics or the study of language." In other words, Sizer notes, even "a seemingly 'solid' college major is not necessarily enough."

Today, there is even more reason to emphasize the need for attracting qualified individuals to the teaching profession. And it is important to make sure that those individuals who *do* choose teaching receive the kind of education they will need to teach the material schools expect students to learn. As Ernest Boyer says, "We cannot prepare the coming generation if the least able students enter the profession. Teaching must become a top priority and gifted students must be recruited." And once students are recruited, colleges and universities must work closely with the schools in preparing curriculum for those who will enter the profession.

A recent Gallup poll indicates that most Americans agree with Boyer's analysis. According to the 1987 poll, 66 percent of the public said that candidates for teaching positions should be prepared both in their subject matter and in teaching theory and methods. Only 29 percent agreed that school districts should hire subject area specialists who have not completed education coursework. In fact, the vast majority of those polled favored *stricter* requirements for teachers than those that currently exist. Seventy percent of the respondents said that prospective teachers should:

- Complete a supervised student teaching experience.
- Pass a paper-and-pencil test covering both their subject area and professional skills.
- Pass a classroom performance test conducted by a trained evaluator.

Need for minority teachers

The Carnegie Task Force on Teaching as a Profession focused attention on a second critical issue in teacher recruitment: the need to attract qualified minority-group teachers. A study by the Educational Testing Service (ETS) predicts that within 10 years, "minority teaching forces will be less than 5 percent, compared to 12 percent in 1980." But by the year 2000, it is estimated that 1 of every 3 students in the U.S. will be a member of a minority group. Because minority teachers serve as role models for minority students and because their presence in the classroom can serve as an important factor in the success of minority students, it is clear that educational leaders will need to pay special attention to increasing the supply of qualified minority group teachers in the coming years.

Promising practices

A number of educational leaders have already begun to implement programs that will help their districts attract qualified teachers. School leaders who responded to the AASA survey for this book indicated that recruiting qualified teachers was a major responsibility. Among the promising practices reported were programs in Arlington, Virginia; Athens, Georgia; and Prince George's County, Maryland.

Cooperation with colleges. The education deans who prepared the Holmes Group's report, "Tomorrow's Teachers," recommended closer cooperation and communication between the universities that train potential teachers and the schools that hire them. To meet this goal, the **Arlington, Virginia,** schools have established the Consortium for Arlington Student Teaching (CAST), an innovative program that combines the resources of university education departments and the school system to prepare teachers to teach at the elementary school level.

CAST student teachers (called "associate teachers") are selected by universities in the year before their student teaching begins. Many of the associate teachers are involved in CAST activities in their schools in the spring. Because associate teachers know their student teaching assignments far in advance, they have more time to prepare for their specific schools.

In a traditional student teaching program, a cooperating teacher and a college instructor both monitor the student. In the CAST program, associate teachers are supervised by "field instructors" (experienced Arlington elementary teachers who have completed additional training in supervision). Because field instructors are considered faculty members at the universities from which their associate teachers come, they effectively fill the role of both the cooperating teacher and the college instructor.

Field instructors work closely with other education professors at three universities currently involved in the CAST program: George Mason University, Marymount University, and James Madison University. As a result, the universities are improving their understanding of what school systems actually *need* and *expect* from student teachers. Field instructors receive college rank and credit toward recertification.

The school district benefits in two ways: first, because qualified student teachers who have positive student teaching experiences in the county are more likely to want to return there as professional staff members. In addition, the district will have the opportunity to influence the curriculum of the education departments that train many of the district's new teachers.

Recruiting minority group teachers. The Clarke County School District in **Athens, Georgia,** has made a special effort to recruit highly qualified black teachers. Each year, the district invites college presidents and deans to visit the school district. "They have the opportunity to look us over," says Associate Superintendent Howard B. Stroud. "They meet with school administrators and community leaders and visit a number of schools."

If the university representatives like what they see, they are asked to encourage their best teacher prospects to visit with the school district. Those teacher candidates who are identified by their universities as the most outstanding are invited to visit the district for two and a half days—at the district's expense. The district guarantees that every applicant will receive at least an initial interview.

Business partnership. The **Prince George's County, Maryland,** public schools, in cooperation with the county's Advisory Council for Business and Industry, has launched an innovative teacher recruiting program to help the county fill an average of 400 teaching slots each year. In 1985, when the program was launched, the county personnel office had a teacher recruiting budget of $4,000—about $10 per teacher.

The business community offered to support the school district's recruiting efforts in two ways: first, by providing financial support for a stepped-up campaign; and second, by offering suggestions drawn from local businesses' efforts in recruiting employees.

To encourage applications, local business representatives accompanied school district recruiters on a recruiting trip to Boston, sponsored a hospitality suite for the district's recruiters, and supported a nationwide publicity effort that even included nationally aired television ads. The number of applicants soared; the district has received about 4,000 completed applications in each of the two years since the campaign was launched.

To encourage applicants who were offered contracts to join the school system, the business community also developed a series of new teacher incentives. Through the program, new teachers are offered discounts on housing (a free first month's rent and waiving the security deposit at a number of apartments—a benefit that may be worth as much as $1,000 to new teachers); discounts on car loans; discounts at restaurants; free checking accounts in local banks; and discounts on moving costs.

Retaining qualified teachers

"It makes no sense to focus on recruiting people," the NGA report noted, "if we don't have strategies to keep them." And there is considerable evidence that there is a real need to retain qualified teachers in the classrooms.

The reports generally agree on three major improvements necessary to retain qualified teachers. These include: raising teacher salaries, improving working conditions, and offering teachers increased responsibilities as they become more experienced.

Raising teacher salaries

Since schools will be competing with other professions to attract and retain the most qualified people, it will be necessary to offer competitive salaries. Today, although local school districts and states have made dramatic improvements in teacher salaries, low pay is still a major concern for school leaders.

- More than half of those who enter the teaching profession leave the classroom within the first five years.
- Linda Darling-Hammond of the Rand Corporation has found that the most academically talented teachers leave teaching at twice the rate of the least able teachers.

Why do teachers leave teaching? The 1985 *Metropolitan Life Survey of Former Teachers in America* found two major reasons: inadequate salary (62 percent) and poor working conditions (41 percent). Specifically, teachers found that too much paperwork, too many non-teaching duties, overcrowded classrooms, and long hours were driving them from the profession.

Theodore Sizer describes the problem this way:

> Our culture signals respect in at least three ways. We give
> people autonomy: We say, we trust you enough to solve

this problem not only for yourself, but for us all. In the
world of work, we dub this autonomy professionalism'. . . . Second, we signal respect with money. We pay
people what we think they deserve. Salary policies are
more complicated than this, of course, but money clearly
is an expression of our priorities. Finally, we signal respect by expressing it: We bestow a Nobel Prize, a
Rhodes Scholarship, a Pulitzer.

Several of the major education reports have urged schools to address
each of these concerns. The Carnegie Task Force recommended that teachers' salaries and career opportunities should be competitive with those of
other professions. NGA recommended that teacher compensation should be
improved both at entry and throughout the teaching career.

In the past three years, many districts and states have made major efforts to raise teacher salaries. In the 1986–87 school year, the NEA reported
that the average *beginning* teacher's salary was $16,000; the average salary
for *all* teachers was $25,313. Since 1982, average teacher salaries have in-
creased 21.5 percent. In the past five years, both Alabama and Arkansas
have passed statewide raises in teacher salaries of more than 10 percent in
each of 2 consecutive years.

These pay increases are an important step in helping schools attract
and retain the best teachers. As the Carnegie Forum pointed out, until very
recently teacher salaries had lost ground to other professions in real dollars.
And even today, when compared with other occupations that require similar schooling and training, educators—both teachers *and* administrators—
rank at the low end of the spectrum.

In surveys conducted by Metropolitan Life in 1984 and 1986, an over-
whelming number of both former teachers (88 percent) and teachers still
in the classroom (94 percent) agreed that "providing a decent salary"
would help "a lot" in retaining current good teachers in teaching.

Restructuring the salary system. Equally important to retaining
qualified teachers is the *structure* of the current salary system. Most pay
scales include 10 or 12 steps. As a result, the Carnegie Forum noted:

Teachers find themselves in their mid-thirties faced with
the prospect of no salary growth in real terms when their
peers are beginning to enter their prime earning
years. . . . The salary structure impels able teachers,
those most likely to raise the performance levels of the
schools, to leave the profession just as they acquire the
experience to assume effective leadership. . . . This country . . . does not enjoy the luxury of deciding whether or
not to spend more; it must decide how much more to
spend and how best to spend it.

What school leaders can do. Obviously, the decision to raise salaries must be made by the board of education and—ultimately—the citizens of each school district. For that reason, this book will not include a detailed analysis of teacher salaries. But educational leaders can play a role in addressing this important issue:

First, they can help their local communities assess how much more they should be spending on teacher salaries—and decide how best to allocate those funds. In some districts, across-the-board pay raises are necessary to make the district competitive with other comparable areas. In other districts, it may be necessary to develop a new salary structure that will encourage experienced teachers to remain in teaching.

Second, school leaders can take action to develop budgets that use available funds to reflect the district's educational priorities. Hiring additional teacher aides to handle paperwork, thus providing teachers with additional time for planning, is one example.

Third, school leaders can communicate regularly with their communities about the costs of quality education. Because education is a highly labor-intensive enterprise that is heavily dependent on the quality and performance of the teaching force, citizens need to know that in education—as in nearly every other aspect of life—you get what you pay for.

Fourth, school leaders can work to involve everyone—students, parents, concerned citizens, college students, alumni, and staff—in the important task of teacher recruiting. There is a role for everyone to play.

Fifth, school leaders can reinforce their district's commitment to quality education. As James Miller and Dennis Sidebottom noted in AASA's report, *Teachers: Finding and Keeping the Best in Small and Rural Districts,* "quality attracts quality. A school district must have a visible commitment to excellence in all areas if it expects to draw outstanding applicants."

There is considerable evidence that a strong sector of the public already understands this. In fact, a Gallup poll conducted in April and May of 1987 found that 54 percent of Americans are willing to pay teachers substantially more than they are currently earning—even if it means raising taxes. How much more? Respondents told the Gallup organization:

- Beginning teachers should earn an average of $20,700.
- Experienced teachers should be paid an average of $31,400.

Finally, school leaders have to let the public know that teachers will be held accountable for salary increases. Strong evaluation programs are an important way to motivate teachers, as the following section discusses in greater detail. But they are also an essential part of building public confidence.

Conditions of work

School leaders cannot make decisions about raising teacher salaries by themselves. But they can make other decisions that may be equally important in retaining qualified teachers. "The push for excellence in education," *High School* states unequivocally, "must begin by confronting those conditions that drive good teachers from the classroom in the first place."

John Goodlad agrees. "The relatively low monetary return for teaching makes it even more urgent to enhance the appeal of teaching as satisfying human work by improving working conditions."

What frustrates teachers? What are the conditions of teaching that teachers find so frustrating? The list, drawn from various reports, is a long one. In many schools and districts, only a few of these conditions may exist. Nonetheless, school administrators can be leaders in eliminating any of these conditions that may be making it difficult for teachers to work:

- Too little preparation time during school.
- Too much time spent on paperwork.
- Requirements that teachers perform such tasks as supervising lunch rooms or monitoring the halls.
- Few opportunities for collegiality.
- Frequent interruptions in class time.
- Little authority to decide curriculum or to select textbooks.
- Too many preparations.
- Student/teacher ratios that are too high.
- Lack of adequate teaching materials.

Recommended changes. One set of recommendations for changing working conditions is included in Boyer's *High School:*

- High school teachers should have no more than four formal class meetings.
- Teachers should have a minimum of 60 minutes each day for preparation.
- Teachers should be exempt from routine monitoring of halls and lunch rooms.

Sizer agrees. He suggests that secondary school teachers should be responsible for only 80 students at a time. "Ways must be found," he says, "to give high school teachers a load that allows them to personalize their work."

Some states and local school districts are moving to deal with these concerns. For example, the American Association of Colleges of Teacher Education reported that the Kentucky legislature approved a bill ensuring reduced class sizes and duty-free lunch periods for Kentucky teachers. The Texas legislature passed a similar bill.

Interestingly, Goodlad notes that there have been "surprisingly few" studies of the working conditions of teachers. One valuable step that school leaders could take to improve working conditions in local school districts would be to conduct a local study. Based on that information, school administrators could develop an action agenda to eliminate the conditions that are most inhibiting to improved teaching performance.

Making many of these changes would not require any significant commitment of money. For example, school leaders might help alleviate teacher isolation by developing a schedule that incorporated a shared planning period for all teachers teaching a given course. Such a schedule would allow more cooperative planning and discussion of common concerns.

Similarly, many teachers are frustrated by the number of interruptions to their teaching day. School administrators who make a commitment to reducing or eliminating such things as public address announcements, pullout activities that remove students from class, or cancelled classes can demonstrate their belief in the importance of what teachers are doing. Improvements like these can lead to a dramatic increase in teacher morale—without major budget expenditures.

Other changes in working conditions might require a change in contractual arrangements between teachers and the school district. The information from a school or district survey could be a helpful tool in those negotiations.

"We know why teachers leave: The primary reasons are low pay and the absence of a professional work environment," the National Governors' Association noted. But if school leaders make teaching more attractive, "we may both slow the turnover and raise the quality of those who enter the profession."

Motivating good teachers

"We know nothing about motivation," Peter Drucker once observed. "All we can do is write books about it."

Drucker's comment, while amusing, is not exactly accurate: There is a growing body of research that shows managers what motivates performance. Ironically, of course, much of the research on employee motivation has revealed the effectiveness of techniques that educators have been using for years to motivate student performance in the classroom:

- Establishing clear and achievable goals.
- Using coaching and communication skills to direct employees toward success.
- Providing regular feedback on how well the employee is doing in meeting these goals.

Although attracting qualified new recruits to the teaching profession is essential in the long term, as *High School* has noted, "Whatever is wrong with America's public schools cannot be fixed without the help of those teachers already in the classrooms."

Salary not necessarily a motivator

What these researchers are finding is that "motivation" and "salary" are *not* synonymous. In fact, while salary can be an important motivator for some teachers, it's probably not as important as many people think.

Many teachers entered the profession understanding that they could not expect to receive high salaries. Goodlad found that 57 percent of those who entered teaching did so because of the nature of the profession itself: the desire to teach in general or to teach a subject in particular (22 percent); the idea of teaching as a "good and worthy profession" (18 percent); and a desire to be of service to others (17 percent).

At the same time, Goodlad also found that, although money was not a major reason teachers gave for entering teaching, "it ranked second as a reason for leaving." He continued:

> We might speculate that, anticipating rewards intrinsic to the work, teachers begin with a willingness to forego high salaries. However, when confronted with the frustration of these expectations, the fact that they sometimes are paid less than the bus drivers who bring their students to school may become a considerable source of dissatisfaction as well.

Bringing teacher salaries up to competitive levels will probably help in retaining qualified teachers. But it may not be useful in *motivating* continued improvements in performance among those teachers who stay. One study by A. Arthur Geis, a management consultant to businesses, found that there are at least three significant problems in using salary alone as a motivator for outstanding performance:

- Employees—and managers—often think that pay is unrelated to job performance.
- Most raises are too small to be effective in motivating employees.
- Pay increases are often affected more by the amount of money available for raises than by the actual performance of employees.

How great a salary increase is required to motivate? Another survey conducted by the *Wall Street Journal* asked employees in more than 3,000 companies about the relationship between pay and motivation. "Pay can be motivating," the *Journal* found, "if the increase is large enough in relation to an individual's income to result in a significant change in financial condition. In order to be effective, such an increase would have to be on the order of 20 to 30 percent."

For many school districts, a pay increase of that magnitude would be difficult to achieve in the short term. A few districts, however, have announced a significant salary increase. The Rochester, New York, public schools have raised the top salary for teachers to $70,000.

Many districts are developing new career paths for teachers. These districts offer experienced teachers increased responsibility—and increased salary—while keeping them in the classroom. Typically, NGA noted, "advancement means moving out of the classroom."

The Carnegie Forum offered a number of recommendations designed to "offer the pay, autonomy, and career opportunities necessary to attract to teaching highly qualified people." The report recommended that schools:

- Restructure the teaching force and introduce a new category of Lead Teachers with the proven ability to provide active leadership in the redesign of the schools and in helping their colleagues to uphold high standards of learning and teaching.
- Make teachers' salaries and career opportunities competitive with those in other professions.

The Holmes Group proposed establishing a three-tier system of teacher licensing. The three levels include:

- **Instructors**—novice teachers whose jobs would last only a few years. "Bright college graduates with a solid academic background in one or two subjects, and who could pass an entrance exam, would be welcome. So would be adults from other professions."
- **Professional teachers**—would consist of educators who had "proven their competence at work, in rigorous professional qualification examinations, and in their own education." These professionals would support and supervise the work of Instructors under the Holmes Group's proposed career ladder.
- **Career professionals**—probably only one-fifth of all teachers would be "top practitioners who can lead their field to improvement." Their role, as envisioned by the Holmes Group, would be "not unlike that of clinical professors in medicine."

Promising practices

Some school districts, however, have established programs that encourage experienced teachers to remain in the classroom. The Napa Valley Unified School District in California has adopted a Mentor Program. The Charlotte-Mecklenburg, North Carolina, schools have instituted a comprehensive career ladder.

Teachers as mentors. The best way to learn how to teach, nearly every expert agrees, is in the classroom. Yet once teachers have mastered techniques that make them effective teachers, they frequently have no way to share their experience with younger teachers. The **Napa Valley, California,** Mentor Program is designed to give experienced teachers an opportunity to share what they have learned with colleagues who are just beginning their careers.

Mentor teachers are credentialed, permanent teachers who are selected by the Board of Education for one-year terms. They are nominated by a selection committee of five teachers and four administrators. The legislation that established the Mentor Program in California provides a $4,000 stipend for each teacher selected. In addition, mentors are supported by $2,000 in administrative money that is used to support the program, to provide substitutes when mentors are out of their classrooms, and for materials.

All first-year teachers are assigned a mentor. In addition, any teacher who has joined the district in the past four years is eligible to call on a mentor teacher. And any teacher in the district can request specific assistance from a mentor teacher in instructional skills, classroom management, or classroom organization. For example, during the 1986–87 school year, Mentor Teachers offered advice on:

- Planning for and using computers during and after school.
- Integrating reading and writing.
- Talking with students about parenting, physiology, and other health education subjects.
- Creating an exciting program for gifted and talented students.
- Choosing appropriate materials for teaching about drug and substance abuse.
- Helping teachers and students take advantage of community involvement programs.

"Each year, experienced teachers make increasing use of the services provided by mentor teachers," says Barbara Pahre. One reason, she believes, is that the mentors' work is not used as a part of a teacher's evaluation. As a result, she notes, "it isn't threatening to ask for help."

Besides the benefits to the teachers who use the services of the mentors, the program also offers benefits to the mentors themselves. The first benefit, of course, is financial. In addition, mentors receive increased job responsibility and increased challenges.

Career ladder. In **Charlotte-Mecklenburg, North Carolina,** a career ladder program offers teachers an opportunity to earn additional salary as they assume increasing responsibilities. Under the program, instituted in 1984 after a four-year planning process, teachers move through six levels: provisional, career nominee, career candidate, career level I, career level II, and career level III. Career level I teachers, for example, are expected to work with beginning teachers. Career level II teachers may assume additional responsibilities for curriculum development.

Each year, teachers develop "action-growth" plans in which they outline specific teaching competencies they want to acquire or improve. They also work with principals and other teacher observer/evaluators to develop a program to meet their goals.

The observer/evaluator teachers are central to the success of the Charlotte-Mecklenburg career ladder. These specially trained teachers make frequent visits to classrooms of all teachers enrolled in the program. They evaluate and rate teacher performance in five areas: management of instructional time, management of student behavior, instructional presentation, monitoring, and feedback.

All newly hired teachers in the district are required to be part of the career ladder program; other teachers are given the option of participating. In 1986–87, 68 percent of the district's tenured teachers did elect to take part in the program.

Response from the tenured teachers who participate in the career ladder has been generally favorable. In one survey, 45 percent of the teachers said they had "stretched, grown, and learned" because of their participation in the career ladder program.

Merit Pay

There was general support in many major education reports for some type of incentive pay program for teachers. For example, in *A Nation At Risk*, the National Commission on Excellence in Education recommended:

> Salary, promotion, tenure, and retention decisions should be tied to an effective evaluation system that includes peer review so that superior teachers can be rewarded, average ones encouraged, and poor ones either improved or terminated.

NGA recommended that teacher incentives should be "align[ed] with schoolwide student performance." The Carnegie Forum recommended that schools "relate incentives for teachers to schoolwide student performance, and provide schools with the technology, services, and staff essential to teacher productivity."

School districts that have instituted such programs today frequently call them "career ladders." These incentive programs often incorporate additional responsibility for teachers, as well as additional salary.

The AASA publication, *Some Points to Consider When You Discuss Merit Pay*, outlines a number of different merit pay programs that are currently operating in schools. These include:

- Giving awards to teachers judged to be good at what they do.
- Giving bonus payments to teachers who accept additional assignments or more difficult assignments.
- Conferring higher status on the "best" teachers in the district, as well as providing them with higher salaries.

- Rewarding teachers who teach others how to be more effective in the classroom.
- Giving extra money to teachers who contract with the district to accomplish agreed-on instructional goals and who accomplish their goals.
- Giving bonuses to all teachers in a school when the students in that school raise their test scores by predetermined levels.
- Allowing teachers to advance on the schedule for completing in-service or college courses.

"Put simply," the publication concludes, "merit pay is any device that adjusts salaries to reward higher levels of performance."

Merit pay programs, which provide financial bonuses but usually involve no increase in responsibility, have decreased during the past several years. During the 1960s, the Educational Research Service (ERS) found that approximately 10 percent of all school districts instituted some type of merit pay program. By 1972, only about 5 percent of districts had merit pay programs in operation. And by 1978, only 1 percent of the nation's school districts enrolling 300 students or more had an operating merit pay program.

Leadership in Action: Teachers

While considering a school or district program to attract, retain, motivate, and reward good teachers, school leaders should address such questions as:

- Is our district likely to face a teacher shortage in the next five years? What will be the causes of that shortage—retirements, resignations, or increasing student enrollments?

- What steps can our district take now to reduce the impact of any potential teacher shortages?

- Why do teachers leave our school or district? What steps, if any, can be taken to reduce the numbers of teachers who leave?

- Does our district offer a competitive salary? What other incentives do we offer teachers? How can we become more competitive?

- How can we improve our teacher recruiting?

- How can we motivate the teachers who are already on our staff?

Chapter 5

Curriculum Leadership

"Perfection of means and confusion of ends seems to characterize our age."

—Albert Einstein

In the past five years, largely spurred on by the education reform reports, American schools have undergone a surge of curriculum reform. As researcher Alan Odden noted in a *Phi Delta Kappan* article:

> The education reform movement has moved faster than any public policy reform in modern history. All the states have expanded their school improvement programs, nearly all have increased high school graduation requirements, most have stiffened college admission requirements, many are deepening the content of course offerings, and many are enacting a variety of policies to strengthen the teaching profession.

The most typical response by state legislatures to the current education reform reports has been to increase graduation requirements. A December 1986 article in *Phi Delta Kappan* outlined some of the changes that have occurred in curriculum since 1980:

- Forty-five states and the District of Columbia have changed their requirements for earning a high school diploma. Generally, these changes have involved increasing the number of courses required for graduation.
- Of the 34 states that had minimum graduation requirements in 1980, all have increased those requirements.
- Six states and the District of Columbia have increased the length of the school year. The California legislature has offered financial incentives to local districts that lengthen their school year.

The findings of the AASA survey for this book confirm that the nation's schools are experiencing dramatic changes in course requirements. In answer to the question, "Has your district changed its course requirements for graduation since 1983—either because of changes in state requirements or because of school district initiative?", fully 84 percent of the respondents said their school district had increased requirements. No respondents indicated their district had decreased requirements. The remaining 16 percent of respondents indicated their district's graduation requirements remained unchanged.

FIGURE 5-1
Changes in Graduation Requirements Since 1983

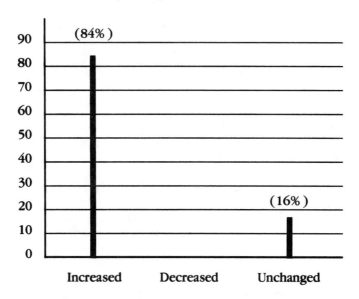

Source: 1987 AASA, Challenges for School Leaders

Who is involved in curriculum reform?

Where have these reforms started? And who has been involved in the process of curriculum reform? Those school leaders in AASA's study who said their district had changed its course requirements for graduation were asked to indicate who had been involved in curriculum changes—and the extent of their involvement.

Administrators have the greatest impact

Responses showed that school administrators were the group most likely to be "significantly" involved with curriculum change.

State legislatures and state departments of education were in second place—slightly more involved than local school boards. State legislatures, state governors, and state departments of education are becoming increasingly important forces in educational reform. Many people today refer to the state legislature as a "super board of education." Whenever the state education agency was involved in curriculum reform, respondents generally indicated it had "significant" involvement. Few respondents indicated that the state was "somewhat" or "not at all" involved.

Local boards of education are the third key player in curriculum reform. Even when reforms were initiated at the state level, most respondents indicated their board of education was "significantly" or "somewhat" involved in curriculum reforms. The tabulations shown in Figure 5-2 reflect the percentages of those who responded to each question. In many cases, figures do not add up to 100 percent—but they give a general indication of who has been involved in curriculum reform.

Clearly there is a great deal of activity at the local and state level. And clearly the publication of various education reform reports has stimulated discussion and action. However, on a most basic issue—What do students need to learn?—there is less agreement among the education reports.

Little agreement in the reports

The consensus of most experts who read the first education reports—*A Nation At Risk, A Place Called School, Academic Preparation for College, High School,* and *Horace's Compromise*—is that they *lacked* agreement on a number of key curricular issues. Here are a few examples of what the reports said about curriculum reforms:

Standards and expectations for students

Many of the reports agreed that schools need to adopt higher performance expectations and higher standards for student achievement. For example, *High School* noted that "for classroom instruction to be effective, expectations should be high, standards clear, evaluation fair, and students should be held accountable for their work." *A Nation At Risk* holds, "Grades should be indicators of academic achievement so they can be relied on as evidence of a student's readiness for further study."

As AASA's *Excellence in Our Schools: Making It Happen* points out, however:

> None of the reports deals adequately with the evaluation/
> certification/eligibility issues in schools. It is one thing to
> raise standards; it is another to develop clear criteria for
> those standards which match learning goals. High
> schools, in particular, structure credit and eligibility systems around time. . . . Consequently, diploma requirements which are stated in terms of courses completed
> rather than outcomes reached may have little bearing on
> the actual learning achievements of students.

FIGURE 5-2
Who Has Been Involved in School Curriculum Reform?

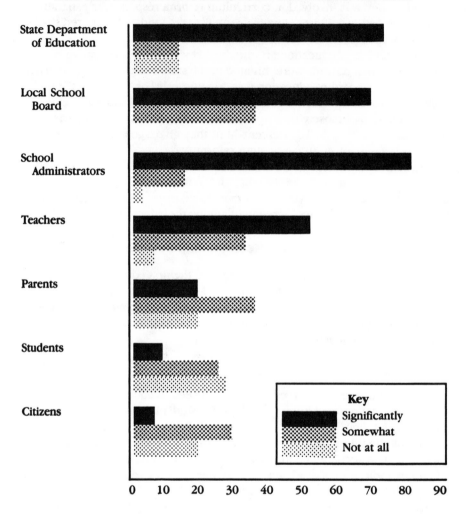

Source: 1987 AASA survey

Only one of the major reports—*Academic Preparation for College*—adopts the approach of emphasizing student *outcomes*. The others all emphasize the importance of taking a specified program of required courses.

Required courses

Even among those that do proscribe a particular course of study, there are dramatic variations in what the authors consider important. Figure 5-3 summarizes the recommendations of five reports: *A Nation At Risk* (listed on the chart as RISK); *High School* (HS); *Educating Americans for the 21st Century* (C-21); *Academic Preparation for College* (PREP) and *A Place Called School* (PLACE).

FIGURE 5-3

Graduation Requirements: What the Reports Recommend

	RISK	HS	C-21	PREP	PLACE
Language Arts	4 yrs.	2½ yrs.	–	YES*	18%**
Mathematics	3 yrs.	2 yrs.	3 yrs.	YES*	18%***
Science	3 yrs.	2 yrs.	3 yrs.	YES*	18%***
The Arts	–	½ yr.	–	YES*	to 15%
Social Studies	3 yrs.	2½ yrs.	–	YES*	to 15%
Physical Education	–	–	–	–	to 10%
Computer Science	½ yr.	½ yr.	½ yr.	–	–
Voc. Education	–	½ yr.	–	–	to 15%
Foreign Language	–	2 yrs.	–	YES*	18%**

Academic Preparation for College does not lay out a specific set of course requirements. It identifies six "Basic Academic Subjects" and sets out what students need to know and be able to do in each.

**Goodlad recommends that all students spend up to 18 percent of their total time in high school studying languages—both English and foreign language. Assuming a student takes 23 courses during high school, he or she could devote 4½ to the study of languages.

***Goodlad recommends that up to 18 percent of a student's time be spent studying mathematics/science.

Other than the general agreement that schools should require more mathematics and science, it is difficult to find much consensus about the *specifics* of changing the curriculum from these recommendations. For example, the arts, listed as a Basic Academic Subject by the College Board, are mentioned only peripherally in *A Nation At Risk*: "The high school curriculum should also provide students with programs requiring rigorous effort in subjects that advance students' personal, educational, and occupational goals, such as the fine and performing arts and vocational education." They are not included in the list of "basic subjects" that the report believes every student should study. Similarly, vocational education, which Goodlad believes should account for as much as 15 percent of a student's required core curriculum, is also virtually ignored in other reports.

What does seem to be emerging from these reports and a plethora of activity at state and local levels, says American Federation of Teachers President Albert Shanker, is a general feeling that adults should take an active role in setting forth what students should study. "We've swung away from the notion that adults had no business in determining what young people need to learn," he notes.

Course content

A second emerging issue, it appears, will be a discussion of *specific* content of the required courses; as well as a more specific look at *how* teachers can best teach this core curriculum to all students. Theodore Sizer notes that it is not enough to say that a school "requires four years of English." "If one asks, *What* English?' the answers flow slowly indeed," he points out.

In 1988, U.S. Education Secretary William Bennett began a discussion of the specific course requirements for secondary school students. His proposed curriculum for a fictitious "James Madison High School" outlines the kinds of books students should read, as well as specific course content for history, literature, mathematics, and science.

Goodlad suggests that most curriculum reform efforts today are misguided because they are directed toward the wrong goals. "What most schools need is not a somewhat lower-level replication of college courses," he points out. Goodlad's researchers, who visited more than 1,000 classrooms, found that the "major shortcoming" of the curriculum today is the failure to train students in the structure and way of thinking for each discipline. As a result, he noted, there is an emphasis on topics, not concepts or principles.

These two areas are related in several important ways as the second phase of the education reform movement begins. There is an opportunity to involve the entire community in a discussion of what the curriculum should include. And there is an opportunity to make sure that discussion is guided by the best pedagogical research. Together, they offer significant opportunities for school leaders to influence curriculum for years to come.

The impact of an educational leader on curriculum

It is important to note that *one* educational leader, with a strong vision and the commitment to making it a reality, *can* have a dramatic effect on the curriculum. Here is just one example. In 1985, the state of California established a curriculum committee to review new textbooks for seventh and eighth grade science courses. The committee rejected all of them because they either ignored the subject of evolution altogether—or watered it down so it was not scientifically accurate.

California State Superintendent Bill Honig followed the recommendations of the committee and rejected the textbooks. In an interview with the *New York Times*, he said, "The issue here is, are we going to allow publishers to water down texts and draft them politically to avoid controversy? Doing so undermines our efforts towards excellence in our classrooms."

If educational leaders are going to affect curriculum change, they will need to do so in the context of what is happening in society. Changes in the economy, for example, already point out the need for reevaluating what students will need to know and be able to do in the future.

The coming information economy

Changes in the American economy will also lead to changes in the curriculum. As the United States moves to what is being called an "information economy," there will be a number of changes that will dramatically affect expectations for students. These will include the following:

- To be successful, those entering the work force will need to have more academic skills than at any time in our history. There will be fewer jobs available for those with limited education and skills.
- Rapid changes in jobs will mean that workers will need to be retrained again and again.
- Workers will need to be generalists who can adapt, rather than specialists who will become obsolete.
- In the information economy, intangibles such as vision and motivation will become even more important. "For the ability of a knowledge worker to contribute in an organization, the values and the goals of the organization are at least as important as his own professional knowledge and skills," says Peter Drucker.

Responding to these changes, says the NGA report, is "not a matter of defining the courses students must take." Instead, it is "a painstaking and continuing inquiry into what skills students should have, and to what degree."

The process of curriculum reform

In *Profiling Excellence in America's Schools*, Roueche and Baker noted one common factor in *successful* curriculum change in these excellent schools: the extensive involvement of teachers in designing and carrying out these important reforms. "Changes and later maintenance don't happen without the support and commitment of teachers, who must 'buy into' the innovation," they noted. They also identified behaviors of educational leaders who want to institute lasting curriculum change:

- They encourage staff-initiated change.
- They provide support, commitment, resources, and enthusiastic participation.

- They initiate changes themselves, consulting with their staffs as they go.
- They follow through to see that the innovation is implemented, evaluated, and modified over time.

Teachers are not the only ones who have a stake in curriculum reform. The entire community should have an opportunity to discuss priorities for education in the future.

One suggestion for community involvement comes from the AASA publication *Excellence in Our Schools: Making It Happen*. A formal "coalition for excellence," the book notes, might involve representatives from several key groups: parents, business and industry, labor, nonparents, educators, government leaders, and others. The result of this effort "should be an appreciation of the important role of education in the community and the need for community support."

One mechanism for thinking about curricular change comes from an article by Fenwick W. English in *Rethinking Reform: The Principal's Dilem-*

FIGURE 5-4
Line Function

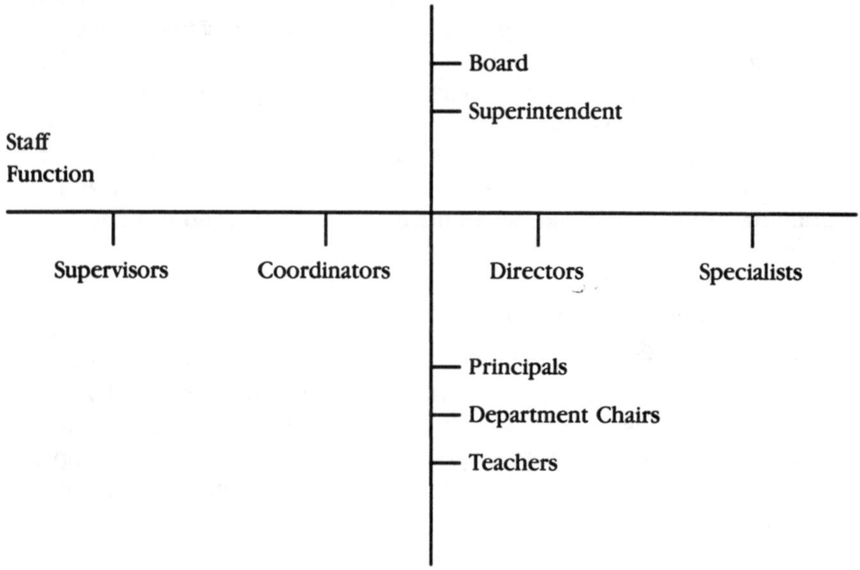

Source: Fenwick W. English, "Who Is In Charge of the Curriculum?" in *Rethinking Reform: The Principal's Dilemma,* Thomas Koerner, ed. (Reston, Virginia: National Association of Secondary School Principals) 1986.

ma. He uses standard business terminology and divides the school system into "staff" and "line" functions. Line functions—performed by teachers, principals, the superintendent, and the board of education—operate the schools and the system on a day-to-day basis. Staff functions—typically performed by supervisors, coordinators, and specialists—support the line.

In the process of curriculum reform, English notes, staff personnel generally have the responsibility for developing the curriculum. "Good practice dictates that staff personnel involve a lot of people in curriculum development . . . teachers to board members."

Figure 5-4 graphically represents, for example, why teachers—who are directly responsible for carrying out the process of curriculum reform—must be involved in the development of new curriculum. Chapter 9 identifies another strategy for dealing with curriculum change.

Leadership in Action: Curriculum Reform

As schools and districts consider curriculum reform, educational leaders might wish to consider the following questions:

● Has everyone in our community been given an opportunity to discuss what students need to know and be able to do?

● How relevant are the recommendations of the education reports for our community?

● Within the broad guidelines established by the state or school district, what are specific learning outcomes for students in each subject?

● How can teachers be given greater responsibility for curriculum development?

● What will be the relationship between staff and line functions in curriculum development?

● What can we learn from past experiences of similar curricular reforms?

● Is there any indication that the proposed curricular reform will occur at the expense of other desirable educational measures or practices?

● Is the proposed curriculum change consistent with what we know about teaching and learning?

● Is the professional staff committed to the proposed reform measure?

────────────────────── *Chapter 6* ──────────────────────

Leadership for At-Risk Students

"A public education system that provides the full range of educational opportunities for all of its children will strengthen our local communities, provide society with trained workers and informed citizens, help improve our productivity and halt our slide into a two-tiered society whose have-nots are needlessly shoved into lives without hope or meaning."

—William Woodside, Chairman
Executive Committee
Primerica Corporation

The students who will provide America's work force for the 21st century are in our schools today. Some educators feel that as many as a third of these children are, based on their current circumstances, at risk of either failing in school, dropping out, or becoming a victim of crime, alcohol or drug abuse, or teenage pregnancy.

In *Innovation and Entrepreneurship,* Peter Drucker observed, "In the 20th century, it is sheer folly to disregard demographics." And demographic changes point to some of the special concerns for school leaders in the future.

The graduating class of the year 2000

A number of demographic trends have combined to heighten school leaders' awareness of the problems of at-risk students. First, there are simply *fewer* children today. U.S. Department of Education statistics show that the population of school-age children has declined from 53.5 million in 1970 to 44.9 million today. The U.S. Census Bureau currently estimates that the birth rate stands at approximately 1.9, less than the 2.1 children needed to replace the population.

Second, more of these children live in circumstances that place them at greater risk for school failure.

In 1987, demographer Harold Hodgkinson, reporting for the Forum of Educational Organization Leaders, noted the following facts:

- 40 percent of the poor in America are children.
- 24 percent of all children live below the poverty level.
- Nearly 60 percent of children born in 1983 will live with only one parent before age 18; 90 percent of these children will live in female-headed families; and a majority will be families with incomes under $10,000.
- The teen birth rate in the United States is *twice* that of any other western nation.
- Today's children come to school speaking over 100 different languages and dialects.
- Nearly 40 percent of all public school students are minorities.
- Since 1960, delinquency rates of young people ages 10 to 17 increased by 130 percent.
- This nation has the highest rate of teenage drug use of any industrialized nation, with over 61 percent of all high school students having used drugs.

A study for the National School Boards Association earlier found that 15 percent of children entering school in 1986 were either physically or mentally handicapped and 10 percent were living with emotional handicaps.

Teen pregnancy: The biggest threat

Teenage pregnancy is the greatest single cause of school drop-out for female students. The Rand Corporation found that 80 percent of students who become pregnant drop out of school—but only 9 percent of female students who are not pregnant become dropouts. The costs—to the individuals and to society—can be staggering. The Center for Population Options estimates that it will cost society $16 billion to support the first-born infants of teenagers over the next 20 years.

Children who do not speak English

Children who do not speak English at home face special achievement problems in school. And the number of such students is increasing. In Arlington, Virginia, for example, the number of non-native English speakers increased to about 30 percent of the student body in 1986–87. Some school districts are so diverse that their student population speaks as many as 100 different languages at home.

Students who do not speak English at home are at special risk of dropping out. The Institute for Educational Leadership (IEL) notes that dropout rates for Hispanic students "are intolerable." Studies show that 25 percent of Hispanic youth are two years behind at the end of the eighth grade. As many as three times as many Spanish language background Hispanic students drop out during or before the tenth grade than do English language background Hispanic youth.

Special problems of refugees

Many of the non-English speaking students are also refugees, who face special problems that affect their ability to function in school. Dalia P. Meza of the District of Columbia Public Schools outlined the characteristics of many of the refugees enrolled in her district:

- A low level of literacy in their native language. Many are non-literate or severely academically delayed. This description often is also true for the parents.
- Poor nutrition—small in stature, poor teeth, skin pallor.
- Non-English speakers—approximately 2 percent speak English fluently, but 79 percent speak no English at all.
- Early teens are often employed during or after school. Adulthood comes early to these children.
- Boys 13 to 16 years of age may have no family, relatives, or permanent residence.
- They or their families frequently move around within the city.
- The families may be divided among several residences.
- They are from rural areas in their native countries. Some come from refugee camps.
- They are children of war/revolution who have lived in fear of soldiers, real bombing, and seeing family members being taken and shot. For many of the children, to have seen dead bodies in significant numbers is not unusual.
- They live in excessively overcrowded housing.
- The head of the household is often a single mother.
- Their parents frequently work two full-time jobs.
- They may have parents who lived here for as long as five years before bringing their children to this country. Long separations from parents are not unusual.

It is the *combination* of demographic trends—the decline in the overall number of children and the increase in the numbers of children with problems that impair their ability to function in school—that has educators worried. In a report published by the Forum of Education Organization leaders, a coalition of 11 major leadership groups, Harold L. Hodgkinson, senior fellow at the American Council on Education, says that the demographics clearly point out the problems many American students are going to face in the years ahead. "These kids are simply going to grow up. . . . It's the only group of kids we have."

Schools and at-risk youth

Not surprisingly, Americans are turning to the schools to solve the problems of these at-risk youth. Many schools have instituted major programs to address the problems of at-risk students. The involvement of the schools is critical, Hodgkinson notes. "The educational system is the only system left that seems to function in a way that we can get a handle on it," he observes.

What can the schools do? Boyer notes that educational institutions "cannot act in isolation." Despite "all its good intentions," he adds, the school "has little influence over home and family environment." So although the school cannot solve the dropout problem by itself, it can take actions designed to reduce the educational problems of these at-risk students.

Examining educational programs for at-risk students

School leaders need to examine their districts' educational practices to determine those that pose the greatest problems for at-risk children and youth. Some of the education reforms already instituted as a result of major education studies such as *A Nation At Risk* have have tended to:

- Increase courses required for graduation.
- Increase the number of proficiency tests required for graduation.
- Reduce social promotions.

Each of these practices has been shown to increase the numbers of students who leave school without graduating. For example, those who advocated increasing academic requirements for all students did not always consider the effect of such a move on students who were having trouble meeting existing requirements. As Ernest Boyer has noted, "Raising the bar doesn't mean more students will be able to jump over it."

Researcher Allan A. Glatthorn examined the implications of the recommendations of the curriculum reform movement—especially increasing graduation requirements—on at-risk youth. He has found:

> Increasing academic requirements is likely to lead to increased failure for at-risk youth. It is likely that additional courses in academic subjects will be taught using the same instructional approaches as those already in the curriculum. Yet these approaches, by their very nature, seem not to be very effective for at-risk youth. The 'best kind' of academic course in the traditional high school program frequently presupposes the ability of students to engage in abstract thinking. For the marginal student who has not made the transition to this type of thinking, instruction seems to be carried out in a foreign language.

The Association for Supervision and Curriculum Development (ACSD) also examined the effect of increasing graduation requirements on all students. The ACSD Task Force on Increased High School Graduation Requirements found both that the most academically able students appear to be least affected by increased graduation requirements and that negative consequences are more likely for high school students who do not go on to college.

Goodlad's extensive study, based on thousands of hours of classroom observation, also led him to the conclusion that for at-risk students, more course requirements might not necessarily lead to better education. He found, for example, that low-track classes frequently include more rote learning; more emphasis on conforming as opposed to independent thinking; lower student satisfaction; less teacher clarity, enthusiasm, and organization; and—from the students' perspective—more punitive and less caring teachers.

Increasing the number of proficiency tests also creates hardships for at-risk students. Studies of school dropouts conducted in Boston and elsewhere have found that school dropouts are more likely to have failed, not taken, or scored low in proficiency examinations than other students. In California alone, 41,000 students out of 98,000 left twelfth grade because they failed graduation examinations or courses needed to graduate, according to a study conducted for IEL.

Finally, ending the practice of social promotions may also create special problems for at-risk students. Studies show that students who are held back actually tend to score worse on achievement tests than similar students who are passed on to the next grade. The IEL report cited a *Harvard Education Letter* study showing that these students have low self-esteem and few friends—factors that ultimately predict school dropouts. Even when students who have been retained are reading as well as or better than their classmates, the Chicago Panel on Public School Finances found, they are 7 to 10 percent more likely to drop out than normal-aged students.

The problems of at-risk youth eventually affect all Americans. The National Education Association (NEA) estimates that businesses spent $350 million in 1985 to teach remedial reading, writing, and math to employees. Taxpayers support unemployment, welfare, and other social services for dropouts and their families. The total cost of these services—and the lost tax revenues from unemployed or underemployed workers—may reach $75 billion per year, NEA data indicate.

Early dropout prevention

Boyer and the IEL both recommend strongly that dropout prevention begin early, "with special emphasis on language, with continuous assessment of student progress, and with skilled counseling." The proven success of federally funded programs such as Chapter 1 has shown that early intervention can help at-risk students be successful in school. Through professional organizations such as AASA and state administrators' associations, educational leaders can serve as advocates for such vitally important early intervention programs.

To counteract the problems of students who have been retained, some school leaders are evaluating their district's promotion and retention policies. They may, for example, organize students in the elementary grades into multi-age groupings. Some are establishing a "transition first grade" program for students who are not ready to make the transition from kindergarten to a full first grade program. Still other districts are promoting students every semester so that those who require remedial work will need to make up only a half year of work. The Seattle Public Schools have limited the number of times any individual student may be retained in a grade to two—one at the primary school level and one at the intermediate level.

Special high school dropout prevention programs. In the high school, there are a number of additional solutions available to meeting the needs of at-risk students. The IEL study notes that dropout prevention for older youth requires a "cohesive, integrated effort" combining the following elements:

- Mentorship and intensive, sustained counseling directed toward the troubled youngster.
- An array of social services, including health care, family planning education, and infant care facilities for the adolescent mother.
- Concentrated remediation using individualized instruction and competency-based curricula.
- An effective school-business collaboration that provides ongoing access to the mainstream economy.
- Improved incentives.
- Year-round schools.
- Heightened accountability for dropouts at all levels of the public education system—schools, school districts, and states.
- Involvement of parents and community organizations in dropout prevention.

Promising practices

The AASA survey for this book found that school leaders are already implementing many of these programs. In fact, respondents included more sample programs for reaching at-risk students than for any other question on the survey. Here are some examples of how school districts are meeting the needs of *all* students.

Peer leadership. In **King of Prussia, Pennsylvania,** peer leaders are used in a program to reach high-risk ninth graders. Students chosen to be peer leaders are successful in school and have achieved recognition in academic or extracurricular activities. They receive training in communication skills, planning, teamwork, and goal setting.

These students then serve as group leaders during a leadership training program held for incoming ninth graders who have had poor attendance, discipline problems, and poor academic records. During the three-day session, held at the Pocono Environmental Education Center, the high-risk students take part in competitive and challenging outdoor activities that emphasize the importance of setting goals, planning, working together, and assuming individual responsibility.

So far, none of the at-risk students who have participated in the program has dropped out. Although "none of the students has emerged as the most exceptional in their grades, they have all been successful," says a school district report on the program. One possible reason for the success of the program is that the at-risk students become part of a community that includes administrators, teachers, and other students. When they are back at school, students have a number of people they can contact for help with in-school problems.

Teenage mothers. In **Arlington, Virginia,** the Family Education Center has been established to deal with the multiple problems of dropouts. This alternative educational program is available by choice to all pregnant students enrolled in the school district. The program is designed to help students:

- Realize their full academic potential.
- Acquire skills required for competent motherhood and family living.
- Maintain good health for themselves and their children.
- Learn about planning future pregnancies.
- Develop vocational skills required for employment and financial independence.

The school district works closely with community agencies—including the Department of Human Services—to provide counseling, prenatal and postnatal checkups, infant care information, and support groups for young fathers and grandparents. The program was identified by the Kellogg Foundation and the American Vocational Association as one of five exemplary programs in parent education.

In general, the program has been successful helping students remain in school. A follow-up study of 1985–86 students, for example, found that 17 had returned to school full-time; 6 were in school and working; 4 had graduated and were working; 3 were working full-time. Only two students had dropped out; three students were not contacted.

In addition, mothers' participation in the Family Education Center program has proven beneficial to their infants. Research by a Georgetown University Hospital physician found that children born to mothers attending the Family Education Center appeared to be in better health and had fewer complications than children of other teenaged mothers.

University partnership. In **Rochester, New York,** the Stay in School Partnership Program is a partnership between the city schools and Nazareth College, with funding from the New York State Education Department. Fifty ninth graders from two of the city's junior-senior high schools participate in the program; twenty graduates from the college serve as tutors.

The program has three goals: to improve student attendance, to build strong academic skills, and to encourage students to stay in school. Tutors are trained in identifying at-risk students, assessing their needs, and designing strategies that will lead them to academic success.

The tutors work individually with students. They can provide tutoring and support for students in four academic areas: math, reading, writing, and social studies. In addition, they are trained to help students with non-academic skills that may help them achieve success in school: improving self-concept, making decisions, solving problems, and planning careers.

Early identification. The **Waupun, Wisconsin,** public schools have developed an extensive program for dealing with students at-risk. For example, the Look-Out Program identifies students with potential problems in "transition years" (sixth and eighth grades) so that counselors in the students' new buildings can monitor their progress and initiate changes if necessary.

The district has also developed a modified curriculum plan for students with academic difficulties. For example, these students may take a one-semester communications course that stresses writing for everyday living, job communication skills, and basic reading skills.

Parents of at-risk students are invited to become actively involved in designing an educational program appropriate for their sons or daughters. They may be involved through home visits, family counseling, behavior monitoring, or in-school conferences. Parents and at-risk students are also provided with information about community resources that are available to help.

Alternative programs. Alternative education programs have been a part of the **Denver, Colorado,** public schools for more than 20 years. The district runs a number of alternative programs, including the Metropolitan Youth Education Centers, created to provide individualized programs for students who have dropped out of conventional schools; and the Byers Alternative Learning Center, created for students who have been disruptive in their home school environments.

At Byers, students are assigned to a "family" grouping of 1 teacher and 12 to 14 students. This family grouping is combined with a strong emphasis on community service and a personalized academic program. The curriculum stresses a "learn by doing" approach and teaches lifelong learning skills such as reading, mathematics, and writing. It also helps students develop interpersonal skills and career skills.

Because teamwork is so important for staff members at Byers, current teachers are active participants in hiring new colleagues. The district notes that this active staff involvement is one of the major reasons for the success of the Byers program. The center serves 100 students, and there is a waiting list.

The Metropolitan Youth Education Centers combine vocational education with academics for students who have reentered school after dropping out. The district is developing an outcome-based curriculum for the program. These centers make special efforts to meet the needs of their students. Some centers have teenage pregnancy programs, for example. At least one has an extended day schedule that includes evening classes.

Promotion and retention policies. The **Seattle, Washington,** public schools have developed an extensive policy statement regarding promotion and retention of at-risk students. Although the policy of the school board states clearly that "students will be promoted to the next school level only when they have achieved a satisfactory level of performance," the district has made a comprehensive effort to ensure the success of at-risk students.

For example, the district requires early identification of at-risk students—by the end of the second quarter for kindergartners. Once students have been identified, parents are notified and are asked to participate in at-home learning activities. Other intervention programs that schools are encouraged to adopt include:

- Pull-out programs, some supported by Chapter 1 funds.
- HOSTS (Helping One Student to Succeed)—individualized instruction provided by community volunteers.
- Using reading resource teachers as consultants for classroom teachers.
- Computer-assisted instruction.
- Changes in instructional approach, methods, techniques, content, or materials.

These programs—and others that are still being developed by school leaders across the country—are vitally important for at-risk students. But they are also important for our entire nation. As David Hornbeck, state superintendent of schools in Maryland, said in an article in *The Washington Post:*

> It used to be the case that the victim of our failure with youngsters was only the youngster. Today, because we need all the kids, we all become the victim. The demographics . . . no longer permit any throw-away or disposable children.

Leadership in Action: At-Risk Students

As education leaders consider school and district plans for meeting the needs of at-risk students, these questions should be discussed:

- How many at-risk students are enrolled in our school/district?

- What do demographic data about our school/district indicate about the numbers of at-risk students in the future?

- What current school/district programs and policies create special problems for at-risk children and youth?

- What resources are available in the school/district and in the community to meet the needs of at-risk students?

- How can we involve families of at-risk students in their educational achievement?

- How can partnerships with businesses or colleges and universities improve educational opportunities for at-risk students?

Chapter 7

Building Partnerships

*"Business's concern for education is based on a powerful
fact of life; education provides us a capable work force,
with communities in which we can live and operate,
and ultimately with a prosperous marketplace."*

—Charles Parry
Chairman and Chief Executive Officer
Aluminum Company of America

O f course, schools do not exist or carry on their work in isolation.
The business community, for example, depends on the schools to
supply a skilled work force—as well as a viable market for future
products and services. (Well-educated people make more money and spend
more.) Citizens depend on the schools to supply a new generation of pro-
ductive workers and informed voters.

Partnership programs are an important way for all those who have a
stake in the schools to make a contribution to them. U.S. Education Secretary William Bennett noted in *First Lessons* that children "must be raised by
the community of adults—all adults." Other major education reports also
stress the importance of partnerships between communities and the
schools. Here is what some of the major reports had to say about the importance of partnerships:

- In *Investing in Our Children,* the Committee for Economic Development, whose membership includes 200 chief executive officers and
  university presidents, stated unequivocally that improving the quality
  of education is "not a cost, but the most important investment this nation can make."

- Although the Carnegie Forum on Education and the Economy, in *A Nation Prepared,* primarily addressed the need for preparing and retaining qualified teachers, the group also discussed the importance of
  school and community partnerships. "Those who would reform from
  the outside and those who would do so from the inside [must] make a
  common cause," the report noted.

- The National Governors' Association also recognized that every citizen needs to be involved with the schools. The NGA report called for "the wider public" to "tap and focus energy and commitment" for improving the schools.
- Ernest Boyer discussed the important learning that can take place outside the schools. "High schools should also establish connections with learning places beyond the schools—such as libraries, museums, art galleries, colleges, and industrial laboratories," he said.
- While examining the status of math and science in American schools, the National Science Foundation (NSF) also recognized the importance of partnerships. In *Educating Americans for the 21st Century,* NSF said that schools "should encourage business and other institutions not primarily involved in education to become active participants and lend fiscal, political, and other support to the local education systems."

Growth of partnerships

Despite the fairly widespread agreement on the importance of public-private partnerships, mechanisms for bringing together those who have a stake in the success of the schools to help improve the quality of education have been slow in developing. Today, this is changing.

In *High School,* Boyer reported that at least 42 states had appointed task forces to study ways to build partnerships between businesses and schools. More than 100 school districts in major cities have established business-education councils. A U.S. Education Department survey in 1984 found more than 46,338 kinds of partnerships operating in 56 percent of the school districts that responded. In general, partnerships today are long-term relationships between the schools and other community institutions.

Today, note John Naisbitt and Patricia Aburdene in *Re-inventing the Corporation,* "American corporations have become this nation's leading education activists." On the local level, businesses provide schools with everything from volunteers to guaranteed jobs for graduates. At the state level, business leaders have been among the strongest advocates for the education reform movement. In South Carolina, for example, business leaders not only were active in developing that state's Education Improvement Act of 1984, but also have been appointed to serve on committees monitoring how well the law is doing. And national corporations have created and sponsored a number of innovative partnerships with schools, many of them described in the 1986 AASA book, *Partnerships: Connecting School and Community.*

Citizens, too, have become more actively involved in the schools. The National School Volunteer Program (NSVP) estimates that school volunteers provided schools with more than half a billion dollars in direct benefits in 1986–87. Only about one-third of current school volunteers are parents, according to NSVP statistics. Approximately one-fourth are retired citizens, and another quarter are college students. Most of the remaining volunteers are business people.

What can partnerships do?

What can partnership programs do? School leaders who responded to the AASA survey for this book reported that partnership programs in their district supported a variety of activities:

- Tutoring.
- Field trips and special activities.
- Donations of supplies and equipment.
- Direct financial support.
- Jobs for students.
- Summer jobs for teachers.
- Loaned executives.
- Resource people for speaking to classes.

Partnership programs described by survey respondents most typically involved businesses. Those findings confirm nationwide studies on partnership programs. In 1983, the last year for which nationwide data is available, the Council of Financial Aid to Education reported that corporations contributed $1.23 billion to education. School leaders also reported that their districts had established partnerships with universities, government agencies, churches, and other nonprofit organizations.

Such partnership programs are vitally important, says Michael Usdan, president of the Institute for Educational Leadership, in a "Viewpoint" article for *The School Administrator:*

> Demographic imperatives should make it abundantly
> clear that educators must broaden their base of support
> to include older citizens, others who are not directly in-
> volved in schools, and the business community, which
> has such great political and economic influence in our
> society.

This chapter outlines a number of important ways that school partnerships enrich educational opportunities. They are divided into five important areas: helping students who are educationally disadvantaged; offering opportunities for enrichment for all students; providing special opportunities for gifted students; helping teachers; and helping prepare students for the world of work.

Promising practices

Helping at-risk students

Chapter 6 has outlined the special educational needs of at-risk students. Across the country, a number of partnerships have been developed to address these concerns.

Here are three examples of partnerships that are successful in meeting the needs of at-risk students:

Providing incentives. One reason that many students drop out of school is their perception that there is no advantage to be gained by remaining a student. In **New York City,** philanthropist Eugene Lang's unique partnership with students in a Harlem elementary school has shown how providing incentives to these students can lead to long-term motivation and achievement.

Through the "I've Got A Dream Foundation," Lang promised to set aside $2,000 toward the college tuition of an entire class of sixth graders—if they successfully completed high school. The Harlem Youth Action Corps agreed to provide intensive support and follow-up for the students. Today, 50 of the original 61 students are still in school and are on schedule to graduate.

Adopt a school. In **Chicago, Illinois,** the story of Harper High School also illustrates the impact of partnership programs on educationally disadvantaged students. The school had traditionally scored near the bottom of all Chicago schools on achievement tests. The dropout rate exceeded 50 percent. Nearly one in four female students became pregnant each year.

When principal Donald Mulvihall approached the Sara Lee Corporation, which had expressed an interest in participating in an adopt-a-school program, his expectations were minimal. "I knew once they heard about our problems, they would want to adopt some other school," he said in *Partnerships.* But the corporation agreed to an initial partnership that involved sending company employees to speak in business classes.

Today the program has expanded to include corporate-sponsored scholarships for outstanding students, grants for teachers to use in the classroom, and scholarships to allow teachers to improve their skills. Reading achievement moved up nine points—"the first glimmer that the hope being pumped into the school by its business partner . . . might be working," it was noted in *Partnerships.*

Boston Compact. In **Boston, Massachusetts,** the Boston Compact is a high-level partnership involving leading Boston employers, the public schools, social service agencies, and local colleges and universities. The program began in part, says William Edgerly, chairman of State Street Bank and Trust, because, "We found out that one-third of the cost of training to help the unemployed was being spent on remediation in basic skills for those who had left school without an elemental grasp of reading, writing, or arithmetic."

The Compact brings together school-based teams of job developers, university professors, and educators working together in a common mission: reducing dropout rates, raising test scores, increasing attendance, and improving academic performance.

Each member of the partnership is committed to certain responsibilities. Colleges offer financial support to the schools—almost $7.1 million in 1985–86, much of it in the form of scholarships to participating institutions. High schools establish programs to reduce dropout rates and increase attendance. Students pledge to meet higher academic standards. And businesses agree to provide jobs for graduates who have met minimum standards in reading and mathematics. Eventually, the goal of the program is to guarantee jobs for *all* Boston students who meet academic requirements for graduation . . . and to guarantee college admission for all qualified Boston students.

The Compact, says William Edgerly, who helped create the partnership while serving as chairman of the Boston Private Industry Council, is "a way of linking improvements in the schools—in attendance and achievement—with employment opportunities in the private sector. . . . Our experience in Boston shows that setting systemwide goals challenges the initiative and ingenuity of the school administration and staff. It works in Boston, and other school systems across the country are increasingly taking this approach."

Providing enrichment opportunities

Partnerships are finding ways to enrich the academic opportunities for all students. Programs include providing state-of-the-art technology to school science and business laboratories, making business employees available for classroom visits and tutoring, and providing increased access to the arts for all citizens. Here are examples of some outstanding partnerships.

Cultural enrichment. In the **CAL Community School District** serving Colter, Alexander, and Latimer, Iowa, a unique partnership has expanded cultural opportunities to the three communities with a combined population of 1,500. Working together with the local chapter of People United for Rural Education (PURE) and the Iowa Arts Council, the partnership brings a seven-performance season of arts productions to students, parents, and other citizens.

Since the program began in 1983, productions have included ballet, jazz, symphony, chamber music, and drama. The school district provides the facilities—a new 230-seat theater—as well as some administrative and clerical support. Volunteers from PURE plan, promote, and staff the performances. The Iowa Arts Council provides grants to supplement the ticket sales.

Computerized access to resources. In **Montgomery County, Maryland,** a computerized data base brings together community resources and students who may benefit from them. The project, organized by the non-profit Montgomery Education Connection, is available to all county teachers. It was designed to offer the business community a simple way to make valuable resources accessible to teachers to enhance the educational program.

The Vitro Corporation developed the program used to manage the data base. The corporation has also donated hundreds of hours to refine the program and train the coordinator in its use. Today, more than 850 resources are listed on subjects that range from trees to tarantulas. For example, a corporate employee whose hobby is wilderness camping has made himself available to speak to classes about survival in the wilderness. He comes to school bringing all his equipment (three tents and various sleeping bags) to emphasize his message that students must be prepared when they enter the wilderness.

The data base also includes a number of other resources. The "personnel" category includes the names of business people who are willing to serve as tutors, mentors, consultants, judges, and speakers. The "materials" category lists instructional aids, surplus equipment, awards, and scholarships available to county students. In a category called "site resources," teachers can learn about student internships, field trips, tours, seminars, and shadow programs. And "teacher opportunities" provides a listing of grants and awards, summer jobs, internships, conferences, and seminars available to the district's teachers.

Teachers can access the information in the data bank by telephoning the Connection Resource Bank. In the future, the organization hopes a computer will be available in each school so teachers can browse through the listings themselves.

Satellite transmission. The **Currituck County** schools serve 2,400 students in a small, rural district on the northeastern coast of North Carolina. As the district tried to strengthen instruction and curriculum, it faced a number of obstacles—including limited resources, difficulties in attracting teachers to a rural community, and the challenges of providing enrichment for gifted students and quality staff development in an area far removed from most institutions of higher learning.

The Distance Learning by Satellite Project—a partnership between the North Carolina Department of Public Instruction, the state Agency for Telecommunications, Appalachian State University, and the school district—has begun to help the district overcome these obstacles. During the pilot year, satellite instruction was used to provide staff inservice. Based on the success of that program, satellite instruction now offers expanded curriculum opportunities for students in 54 rural schools.

Computers in the classroom. In **Blue Earth, Minnesota,** partnership efforts have supported a computer learning program that benefits every student in the district. Four years ago, local business people agreed to help the school district raise money to support a computer coordinator. In a rural community of only 4,200 citizens, local businesses quickly responded with pledges of more than $60,000 over a three-year period. Telex, the community's largest corporation, was a major contributor; but donors also included local doctors, lawyers, and other Main Street businesses.

When the state legislature was evaluating school districts in a grant program designed to find ways to demonstrate the effective use of technology in education, Blue Earth's commitment to computer education was one factor in the district's selection as a demonstration site. And that grant, in turn, brought the district to the attention of Apple Computers, searching for some ways to experiment with a concept they call the Classroom of Tomorrow.

What will the classroom of tomorrow look like? If the Blue Earth schools are any indication, it will be a school in which every student has a computer on his or her desk all day . . . and another computer at home for homework. Major contributions from Apple are making that classroom a reality, says Suzan Sollie, Apple Classroom of Tomorrow coordinator for the school district. Today, all 140 students in grades 5 and 6 have a computer on their desks. Teachers in grades K through 4 share a computer lab that can accommodate an entire class of children at one time. In the high school, the primary use of computers is for teaching writing, and there is a computer lab dedicated to that purpose. Two other fully equipped labs offer teachers the opportunity to use computers in business education, math, and computer science.

"One partnership leads to another," Sollie notes. "Today, our school district is forming a number of creative partnerships with software companies as a result of our involvement with Apple." Those partnerships, she estimates, have provided the district with more than $100,000 in software over the past three years.

Opportunities for gifted students

Meeting the educational needs of America's most gifted students is vitally important if our country is going to maintain its competitive position in the world economy. A number of partnership programs have developed ways to enrich educational opportunities for these students:

Promoting the arts. In **Littleton, Colorado,** the Littleton National Bank sponsors an art contest for local elementary and secondary school students. Each grade is assigned a specific month to illustrate—kindergartners illustrate December, for example. Teachers collect the art work, which is graded by a panel of local artists who have worked with children at all grade levels.

The bank awards three prizes in each grade. The first-prize winners are then published in a full-color calendar distributed by the bank to citizens in the community.

Fostering math and science education. Boyer's *High School* outlined a number of partnerships that focus on students gifted in math and science. Monsanto, for example, invites advanced mathematics students from St. Louis' Southwest High School to receive supplemental computer programming instruction. One student said after the visit, "I met and learned from three successful black engineers. They were all young and attended different schools. They set an example for me that I can pattern myself after."

Helping teachers

Some of the most successful partnerships have looked at ways of motivating and renewing teachers. Both universities and businesses have launched successful programs that help districts attract, motivate, and retain qualified teachers.

Teachers institute. In **New Haven, Connecticut,** the Yale-New Haven Teachers Institute is supported by Yale University, the National Endowment for the Humanities, and a number of area foundations. Each year, 80 teachers from the New Haven public schools are enrolled as Fellows of the Teachers Institute. They attend a number of talks and seminars, conduct independent research, prepare curriculum, and submit a written evaluation of the program.

Seminars—which include topics in English, history, science, mathematics, art, and other disciplines—begin in the spring and continue through July. Teachers then plan and develop curricular units using the research facilities of the Yale libraries and the information they learned in the seminars. Since the program began, more than 300 curricular units have been developed for the public schools.

Each Fellow receives a stipend at the conclusion of the Institute. The bigger payoff, say the teachers, is the increased prestige and excitement they have gained as a result of their participation.

Teacher mini-grants. In **Littleton, Colorado,** a partnership with the Honeywell Corporation supports the Teacher Venture Fund which awards mini-grants to teachers. These small grants, ranging from $100 to $250, provide "risk capital to entrepreneurial teachers who want to develop new ideas to enrich student classroom experience," says the district.

Introducing students to the world of work

Another innovative area of partnership has been programs that connect companies with the classrooms. In some of these programs, the connection is made primarily through teachers—businesses supply experts to serve as instructors in math or science classes, for example. In other programs, businesses reach out directly to students, inviting them to find out first-hand about careers.

Exploring careers. In **Seattle, Washington,** the Private Initiative in Public Education (PIPE) program has established a number of partnerships designed to introduce students to the world of work. On Student Exploration Day, students from 13 schools were invited to spend a day learning first-hand about a number of careers.

At the Providence Medical Center, for example, students and their parents were conducted on a tour through 14 departments. At the *Seattle Times,* aspiring journalists shadowed veteran reporters and even had the opportunity to cover a meeting of a school board committee. And at Northern Life Insurance, students learned how to print out computer graphics.

"Without this link, the heart might go out of business and the city itself," says Rachel Imper, manager of corporate public relations for Northern Life Insurance Company. "At the same time that we're helping students better prepare themselves to become quality employees, this mutual sharing makes Seattle a nicer place to do business."

Science and technology high school. In **Fairfax County, Virginia,** local science and technology businesses raised more than $1 million in cash and equipment to launch the county's new science and technology high school. Donors to the school include national corporations such as Mobil, AT&T, Honeywell, Boeing, and Exxon. But local businesses such as C&P Telephone have also served as corporate sponsors.

When the labs were being developed, says Lynford Kautz, executive director of the Fairfax County Public Schools Education Foundation, businesses were invited to work closely with the school system to outline the curriculum that was needed to develop scientists for the new high-tech businesses that are becoming an increasingly important part of Fairfax County's economy. They were also challenged to provide the equipment for those laboratories. "It was both an opportunity and a challenge."

Once the laboratories were installed, business people worked closely with the schools to train teachers in using the state-of-the-art equipment for such disciplines as biotechnology, telecommunications, and energy science. In many cases, they have continued a working relationship with those teachers today.

"Business is committed to upgrading the overall quality of education in Fairfax County," said Mel Perkins, general manager of engineering at AT&T and former chairman of the Superintendent's Business/Industry Advisory Council. "We all live in this community, all our employees live here, and many have children going to the local schools. We want a quality environment."

Leadership in Action: Partnerships

As your district considers adopting or expanding partnership programs, here are some questions you may wish to consider:

- What are the educational priorities of our district?

- Who in the community shares a particular interest in helping the district reach specific goals?

- How can a partnership benefit both parties?

- What policies and guidelines have we developed for partnerships?

- How can we turn partnerships into ongoing relationships?

- What staff are needed to develop and maintain partnerships?

Chapter 8

Involving Parents

"The family is critical to success in school."
—U.S. Department of Education

"You are your child's first—and most important—teacher," begins AASA's *Parents . . . Partners in Education,* a booklet about parent-school interaction. A number of recent research studies have confirmed the vital importance of parent involvement in education.

The U.S. Department of Education summarized research on effective educational programs in *What Works: Research About Teaching and Learning.* In noting the results of studies that were "consistent, persuasive, and fairly stable over time," the department found an important theme emerging in studies of parent involvement:

> The 'curriculum of the home' is twice as predictive of academic learning as family socioeconomic status. This curriculum involves informed parent-child conversations about everyday events, encouragement and discussion of leisure reading, monitoring and joint analysis of television viewing and peer activities, deferral of immediate gratifications to accomplish long-term goals, expressions of affection, interest in the child's academic and other progress as a person, and perhaps, among such unremitting efforts, occasional doses of caprice and serendipity. The evidence suggests that parental influence is no less important in the high school years.

Those results should not surprise anyone. After all, children spend only about 13 percent of their waking hours of their first 18 years of life in school and 87 percent of their waking time under the nominal control of their families.

The curriculum of the home

What elements make up "the curriculum of the home?" Perhaps the most important is holding high expectations. One National Institute of Education study by Rhoda McShane Becher examined a number of research reports on the effects of parental aspirations on student achievement. The report concluded:

> Children with higher scores on measures of achievement, competence, and intelligence had parents who held higher educational expectations and aspirations for them than did parents of children who did not score as high. Parents of the former children also exerted more pressure for achievement, provided more academic guidance, and exhibited a higher level of general interest in their children.

A study by educational researchers Robert Albert and Mark Runco followed two groups of gifted 12-year-old boys, all with similar family backgrounds and family incomes. About half had IQ scores of 150 or more; the other half scored in the 99th percentile in math-science achievement. The researchers found that *involvement of parents*—including discussing homework and discussing television programs or reading—was the highest predictor of high IQ and clearly tied to the boys' creative achievement.

Benjamin Bloom's research team reached the same conclusion in *Developing Talent in Young People,* a study of "world-class" achievers in athletics, academics, and the arts. One of the most striking conclusions of the study was the vital importance of parent expectations and parent involvement in the subsequent success of these young achievers. "In the majority of these homes," Bloom wrote, "we found that the parents placed great stress on achievement, on success, and on doing one's best at all times. These parents were *models* of the 'work ethic.'" In addition, the report noted that family routines—including meals, bedtimes, family activities, and recreation—"were structured to give the children appropriate responsibilities and to help them become 'self-disciplined.'"

In *The Evidence Continues to Grow: Parental Involvement Improves Student Achievement,* Anne T. Henderson summarized nearly 50 studies of parental involvement. She concluded:

> Programs designed with strong parent involvement produce students who perform better than otherwise identical programs that do not involve parents as thoroughly, or that do not involve them at all. Schools that relate well to their communities have student bodies that outperform other schools. Children whose parents help them at home and stay in touch with the school score higher than children of similar aptitude and family background whose parents are *not* involved. Schools where children are failing improve dramatically when parents are called in to help.

Benefits for all students

It is important to note that parent involvement is an important way to improve educational performance of *all* students—regardless of their family income. Researchers R.J. Gigliotti and W.B. Brookover made a special effort to reduce or eliminate the effects of family income in their study of parent participation in education. They studied pairs of schools with similar size, geographic locale, and family income. They found that *parent participation*—not parent income—was critical in determining the overall effectiveness of schools.

Researcher Herbert Walberg looked at one inner-city Chicago school in which parents and teachers are working together to promote the best possible education for the school's students. Everyone—parents, teachers, administrators, and students—signs a contract spelling out specific responsibilities. For example, parents promise to provide a quiet, well-lit place for study and to enforce regular study hours. The results "show that inner-city children can make middle-class progress in achievement if educators work cooperatively with parents in pursuit of joint goals," Walberg noted.

Elements of parent involvement

What does "parent involvement" mean? *A Nation At Risk* outlined a number of specific steps that parents can take to help their children's performance in school. These include:
- Encouraging their children to study.
- Discouraging satisfaction with mediocre performance.
- Encouraging good study habits.
- Encouraging their children to take more demanding courses.
- Nurturing their children's curiosity, creativity, and confidence.
- Exhibiting a commitment to continued learning themselves.

Walberg reviewed more than 2,500 studies of what he calls "educational productivity." He noted that although evidence "suggests that the efficiency of the home in fostering learning has declined for several decades, the cooperative partnerships between the home and the school can dramatically raise educational productivity." Walberg also suggested a number of specific steps parents can take to improve student achievement:
- Providing books and a place for studying.
- Observing routines for meals, bedtime, and homework.
- Monitoring the amount of time spent watching television.
- Limiting the hours for after-school jobs.
- Discussing school events.
- Helping students meet deadlines.

Moreover, this type of parent involvement, Walberg noted, helps both individual students *and* the overall student body achieve at a higher level than might otherwise be expected.

There are a number of other, more substantive, ways that parents can become involved with their children's education. These include helping their children with at-home learning activities, participating as a school volunteer, and serving on school policy or governance committees or councils. In a 1982 *Educational Leadership* article, Barbara Tucker Cervone and Kathleen O'Leary developed a continuum of parent involvement activities. The article outlines a number of ways that schools may involve parents in their children's education—both as passive participants and as more active decision makers. For example, sending home good news notes, sponsoring an open house, or establishing a parent bulletin board in the school are ways to inform parents about school activities without expecting active involvement. Involving parents as classroom volunteers, asking parents to serve on advisory committees, or developing at-home learning activities are more active ways to include parents in their children's education.

The importance of home-school communication

One of the most important—yet most often overlooked—components of parent involvement in education is communication between parents and schools. Parents need accurate information about their children's education if they are going to be able to make sound judgments about the education their children are receiving and if they are going to be active participants in their children's learning. Schools need accurate information about students if they are to be able to design programs that meet their educational needs. And *both* schools and parents need communication programs because they tend to build public support for the schools. Yet unfortunately, effective communication programs are still lacking in some schools and districts.

Surprisingly large numbers of parents are excluded from some of the most common, traditional communications from the school. Epstein noted that, in one survey included in the *Encyclopedia of School Administration and Supervision,* over one-third of the parents reported they had no conference with the teacher during the year. Almost two-thirds never talked with a teacher by phone. Although most teachers (over 95 percent) reported that they communicate with parents of their students, most parents said they were not involved in deep, detailed, or frequent communications with teachers about their child's program or progress.

An article by Juleen Cattermole and Norman Robinson in *Phi Delta Kappan* compared the way parents *actually* learn about their children's schools and the ways in which they *preferred* to learn about those schools. They note that "parents clearly like to rely on first-hand sources of information." Although parents ranked friends and neighbors among the 10 most likely sources of information about the schools, the authors note, "they did not rank them as highly preferred sources." Instead, parents prefer information that comes to them directly from the schools—through their children (still the number one source of information), their children's teachers, and through report cards and school newsletters.

Promising practices

School leaders who have not already done so need to establish *regular, two-way* communication programs between schools and parents. Such communication is important at *every* level—the classroom teacher, the building principal, and the school superintendent all need to establish regular methods of communicating with parents. Here are some examples:

Parent publications. In **Atlanta,** the APPLE Corps (Atlanta Parents and Public Linked for Education) publishes and distributes *A Citizen's Handbook and Academic Calendar for the Atlanta Public Schools,* which provides information on how the schools work: who to call for what; what goes on when; and what programs are available to students. Weekly calendar pages are interspersed with educational quotes and photos. Other school districts publish wall calendars that include specific information about school vacations and inservice days, school policies and procedures, important telephone numbers, and special events.

Parent advisory councils. In *High School,* Boyer writes about attending a meeting of the Advisory Council at a high school he called "Garfield High"—a comprehensive high school "in the middle of one of the largest and most distressed cities in the United States." Such advisory councils include parents, teachers, and the principal, and meet regularly to discuss such topics as school security, grading, parent-teacher conferences, and extracurricular activities. *High School* recommends that a Parent-Teacher-Student Advisory Council be established at every secondary school in the nation.

Weekly parent letters. At Belle View Elementary School in **Fairfax County, Virginia,** second-grade teachers have printed special stationery featuring an ice cream cone and the logo, "Here's the Scoop From Grade 2." Every week, teachers send home a handwritten note outlining important achievements for the week and outlining upcoming activities.

Parent conferences. In **Indianapolis, Indiana,** the school district and the business community cooperated on the Parents-In-Touch project, aimed at getting *every* parent in the school district to attend parent-teacher conferences twice each year. Business leaders work through civic and professional organizations to encourage employers to release their employees to attend conferences. Schools make special efforts to communicate with parents about the conferences and schedule special teacher working hours so parents who are not released from their jobs can attend conferences after work.

Encouraging attendance at parent-teacher meetings. To encourage working parents to attend parent-teacher association meetings, some schools sponsor pot-luck dinners that the entire family can attend. After the dinner, children go to one room to watch a movie, parents and teachers stay together to conduct important school business.

At-home learning activities

One of the most important research findings on parent involvement is the importance of involving parents in at-home learning activities. The Home and School Institute (HSI) of Washington, D.C., has been a leader in developing such approaches. Their experience, according to HSI Director Dorothy Rich, is that "priority attention should be given" to involving parents in their children's learning. "This is the basic, most fundamentally meaningful form of participation from which other modes can flow."

Parents are willing to become involved with their children's education in this way. Joyce Epstein of Johns Hopkins University's Center for Research on Elementary and Middle Schools found that more than 85 percent of parents said they spent 15 minutes or more helping their child at home when the teacher requested their help. Such programs, Rich notes, appeal "to the most basic parental motivation for involvement in the first place—the desire to help one's child do better."

At-home learning fits the schedules of today's parents, who frequently are both employed outside the home. Many school administrators have been frustrated in their attempts to organize meetings for parents . . . even when those meetings are held in the evenings. A number of researchers have found that working parents do not miss these meetings because they are uninterested in their children's education, but because they prefer to spend the limited time they have available with their children.

A study by Jean Wellisch outlines the vital role of school administrators in promoting parent involvement in education. Her study found that parent involvement was one of the factors that affected reading and math achievement. What led to parent involvement? Researchers found that parents were significantly more likely to participate in schools where administrators assumed more responsibility for policy decisions—especially decisions about the school's parent involvement program.

Parental choice

A useful first step is to survey parents—and the community at large—about their goals for the district's schools. Such a survey can help identify both strengths and weaknesses of current programs. The survey results can also be used to build consensus for making changes.

School administrators also need to increase their efforts to involve parents and community members in discussions and decisions about school policies. A number of surveys, including the 1987 Gallup Poll on American

Education, indicate that parents are *willing* to participate in such discussions and are more likely to *support* policies they believe they have had a part in determining.

One of the most controversial recommendations of the NGA Report concerned not just parent *involvement* in education, but parent *choice:*

> Expand opportunities for students by adopting legislation permitting families to select from among kindergarten to twelfth grade public schools in the state. High school students should be able to attend accredited public postsecondary degree-granting institutions during their junior and senior year.

The report noted that many states have already moved to incorporate some parent choice. These include:

- **Arizona**—Students are permitted to attend school in a district other than that in which they reside. State funds follow the student from one district to another. Inter-district transfers are not permitted if they will have a negative effect on integration and desegregation. Students are also allowed to receive high school credit for courses taken at junior colleges or universities. School districts do not lose funds if students take these courses.
- **Minnesota**—Since 1985, high school juniors and seniors have been permitted to take courses at colleges and universities and in vocational-technical programs.
- **Massachusetts**—The state education department helped survey parents about the most popular types of programs in a particular district and then provided planning time for faculty members to establish various programs. The state provides some transportation funds for minority students who live in Boston and Springfield so they may attend public schools in neighboring suburbs.
- **Colorado**—The "Second Chance Program" permits high school students who have not succeeded in their present public school to transfer to another district to attend a program geared to them. In the first year, about 150 students participated in this program.
- **Florida**—School districts and community colleges are encouraged to work together. In many districts where such partnerships have developed, high school students are permitted to take courses offered by the community college for credit. Several thousand Florida students participate in this program each year.

Proponents of such programs suggest that increasing parental choice will increase parental involvement and commitment to the schools. Others express reservations. Manya Ungar of the National Parent Teacher Association said, "We believe that *every* school should have strong curricula, that *every* school deserves highly qualified and well-compensated staff, and that *every* school ought to be delivering adequate instructional materials" (emphasis added).

Concerns about parental choice. Two of the biggest concerns about such programs are *equity* and *access.* In a major study of choice programs conducted by the New World Foundation, titled *Choosing Equity,* researchers found a number of potential problems in choice programs:

> An open enrollment system which does not equalize resources, mandate open admission and retention, expand guidance services for parents and students, and simultaneously upgrade the quality of comprehensive schools can become another mechanism for stratification and segregation.

Major questions need to be resolved before any large-scale program of parental choice within the public schools is implemented. These include:

- Will families of all income levels and from all geographic areas really be able to participate fully in a program of parental choice? Or will limits on transportation funds prohibit some students from full participation?
- What will happen to rural schools? Will choice programs drain off the best students?
- How will racial balance be affected? What safeguards can be built into the program to ensure that choice programs do not resegregate the schools?
- How will choice programs affect students who are not successful in more traditional public school programs? Will special efforts be made to develop programs for these at-risk students, or will they be ignored?

Because of these concerns—most of which have not been successfully addressed in any large-scale program of parental choice—many school leaders still have serious reservations about such programs. At the same time, school leaders recognize that such programs are appealing to some governors and state legislators who often assume increased importance in establishing educational priorities.

Certainly some choice-promoting programs hold out more promise than others. Programs that encourage schools to develop specialties—a science and technology emphasis in one school, an arts emphasis in another—can provide effective ways to use students' interests to meet their educational needs. Magnet schools are an excellent example.

For example, the Los Angeles County High School for the Arts opened in 1985 to students who want to pursue a career in the visual or performing arts. More than half the students enrolled are minority students. They study a curriculum that includes both academic subjects and also concentration on their art discipline. The first graduating class scored higher than any other high school in Los Angeles County on the California Assessment Program test of basic skills.

Before a statewide program of parental choice is mandated by the legislature, educational leaders might be wise to consider better ways to promote parent involvement and choice in their own school systems. These locally developed programs can be designed to meet the needs of a school district's students. They should also be sensitive to concerns over equity and access.

Parents should be regularly involved in discussions with school administrators and other policy makers. The National Committee for Citizens in Education has outlined a number of effective ways that parents can participate in such discussions. Many are contained in the aptly titled, *Beyond the Bake Sale.*

Parents are, as Dorothy Rich of HSI says, the "forgotten factor" in education. One of the challenges facing school leaders during the next decade will be to find ways to use the valuable resource that parents provide. School districts that do *not* find new ways to involve parents in their children's education and to provide alternatives within individual schools . . . may find that these decisions will be made for them by the state legislature.

Leadership in Action: Involving Parents

As schools or districts discuss ways to involve parents, school leaders may wish to consider the following questions:

- In what ways are parents involved with our educational program today?

- What are the benefits to our school/district from parental involvement?

- How else might the district and our schools involve parents?

- What training do we provide for teachers and administrators in the importance of parental involvement, as well as on how to involve parents in their children's education?

- What priority do we place on formal evaluation instruments on involving parents in their children's education?

- How can we involve parents in at-home learning activities?

- What choices can or do we give parents?

Chapter 9

Leadership Beyond The Reports

"But above all, try something."

—Franklin D. Roosevelt

Despite the wave of education reform that has taken place during the past five years, there still remain substantial challenges for American public schools. Many of them—providing more and better-trained teachers, meeting the needs of at-risk students, involving parents and the business community in education, developing new curricula—have been discussed in this book. Bringing about these needed changes—and others not yet anticipated—will require transforming leadership.

The recommendations for change included in the major education reports are daunting. Implementing all of them will call for a dramatic restructuring of what schools teach, how they teach it, and how they are organized. Where can a school leader begin? Peters and Waterman outline a number of specific steps to follow:

- Focus immediately on tangible results—rather than programs, preparations and problem-solving—as the first step.
- Identify one or two specific short-term goals for which the ingredients for success are already in place.
- Focus on what *can* be accomplished, not what *cannot*.
- Focus on what people are ready to do now.
- Once one project has been successfully completed, ask those who were involved with it their ideas on how to follow it up.

AASA's publication, *Excellence in Our Schools: Making It Happen,* proposes a "discrepancy model" for effecting educational change. That model has been used in developing many of the checklists and suggestions contained in this chapter.

Step 1: Where are we now?

Before beginning any major educational change, it is wise to assess current conditions. Considering the issues identified in this book, as well as specific information about local schools and conditions, school leaders might begin the process of change by assessing their own school or district's strengths and weaknesses.

Community surveys, discussed in Chapter 8, are an important tool in assessing a district's strengths and weaknesses. Formal and informal discussions with parents, teachers, and community members can also provide valuable information about how the school district is perceived in the community.

What are our strengths?

Every district has "lighthouse" teachers, programs, or schools. Identify the strengths of your school or district.

A. _____

_____

_____

B. _____

_____

_____

C. _____

_____

_____

D. _____

_____

_____

E. _____

_____

_____

What are our weaknesses?

Identify areas in the school/district that need improvement. This book has outlined a number of specific areas for consideration, including shared decision making; recruiting, retaining, and motivating teachers; curriculum; at-risk students; partnerships; and involving parents. After reviewing information in this publication, you may wish to identify specific concerns about this issue as it relates to your district (for example, "We need to address the problem of teenage pregnancy and its effect on at-risk students in our district").

A. _____

_____

_____

B. _____

_____

_____

C. _____

D. _____

E. _____

Step 2: Setting priorities

Yogi Berra said it best: "If you don't know where you're going, you might not get there." After identifying strengths and weaknesses, select an area or areas that should receive priority.

_____

What are we actually doing now in our schools that contributes to effectively dealing with this issue? Be specific about programs and plans that now exist. Do not include any program or activity that cannot be documented.

A. _____

B. _____

C. _____

D. _____

E. _____

F. _____

G. _____

What could we be doing to deal more effectively with this issue? Again, be as specific as possible.

A. _____

B. _____

C. _____
   _____
D. _____
   _____
E. _____
   _____
F. _____
   _____
G. _____
   _____

Step 3: How do we get there from here?

Identify specific steps that can be used to deal with the issue you have identified. Identify person(s) responsible for carrying out these action steps, a
time by which these steps should be accomplished, and how the cost, if any,
will be assumed.

Specific steps in action plan	Person(s) responsible	Time line	Cost
A.			
B.			
C.			
D.			
E.			
F.			
G.			
H.			

This chart can help you develop a specific plan of action to address the
priorities you have identified. But, as General Gavin once noted, "Nothing
chastens a planner more than the knowledge that he will have to carry out
the plan." To turn your plan into a reality, it will be necessary to make the
following judgments:

Cost: Will there be costs associated with the specific action steps you have identified? Where will the funds to support these activities come from? If the costs of the action step are greater than the perceived benefit, you will have to reconsider the strategy or eliminate it from the action plan.

Responsibility: Who will be responsible for carrying out the action steps? Do school personnel need to assume full responsibility? Can parents and community members be involved? Can a community partnership help address the concern? Who will be responsible for following up to ensure that the person or group with the responsibility for carrying out the action step has followed through?

Time line: Successful objectives are:
- Realistically attainable
- Measurable
- Attainable within a specific time frame.

The "time line" section of the chart can help establish the sequence in which each action step needs to be completed. It can also provide benchmarks for measuring your district's success in achieving its objectives.

Obstacles and modifications

Are there any obstacles that may have to be overcome in carrying out your action plan? Be harshly realistic in outlining those obstacles. Discuss possible modifications that may need to be made to your plan in view of the obstacles you have identified.

A. _____

_____

_____

B. _____

_____

_____

C. _____

_____

_____

D. _____

_____

_____

E. _____

_____

_____

Resources

What resources does your school or district have that can be tapped to address the problem? What resources are available in your community? How can your school and community work together to develop an action plan to deal with your school priorities?

Resources of school district	Resources of community
A. _____	A. _____
B. _____	B. _____
C. _____	C. _____
D. _____	D. _____
E. _____	E. _____

Communication

Who needs to know about the priority for your school or district? What methods of communication are best able to reach that target audience?

Target audiences	Communication vehicles
A. _____	A. _____
B. _____	B. _____
C. _____	C. _____
D. _____	D. _____
E. _____	E. _____
F. _____	F. _____

What communications plan is already in place for the district? What modifications or changes to that communications plan will need to be made in order to achieve the district's goals?

A. _____

_____

_____

B. _____

_____

_____

C. _____

_____

_____

D. _____

_____

_____

E. _____

_____

_____

Communication plays a vital role in the process of fostering continual change. Specifically, it requires a commitment to do two things:

1. Honor, in any way possible, any valuable, completed action by people at all levels of the organization—especially those who meet directly with customers.
2. Seek out a high number of opportunities for swapping success stories.

Communication is particularly important for school leaders because they are responsible to so many constituencies. As this book and others have pointed out, public elementary and secondary education will require increased cooperation and support from parents, the community, business and industry, all levels of government, and colleges and universities.

Consider choosing a theme for your campaign. This "mission statement" can be a way to focus attention and rally support for your efforts. IBM, for example, has adopted a statement by founder Thomas Watson as its mission statement: "We want to give the best customer service of any company in the world." All plans for new IBM products or services must contribute to that mission. Similarly, a theme for your school district can provide a clear, understandable way to communicate your district's priorities.

Leadership for learning

Building the needed consensus for the changes outlined in this book—

and others that are identified in individual schools and districts—will require all the skills of a successful school leader:

- **Long-term thinking**—in bringing together key decision makers from throughout the community to plan for the future.
- **Relationship with the outside**—to understand the coming changes in society and in education, to determine how those changes are likely to affect local schools and school districts, and then to establish a plan of action to meet those challenges.
- **Vision**—to create and articulate a dream of what the school or district might be like in 5 or 10 years, and then to continue to emphasize that vision.
- **Outstanding management skills**—to keep the schools running on a daily basis, and to make sure that the decisions that are made are the *right* decisions . . . those that carry out the mission of the school or district.
- **Communication/political skill**—to bring the various constituencies in to support the vision of the future.
- **Renewal**—to build in the process of continual change.

"The very concept of leadership," Arthur Schlesinger, Jr., has noted, "implies the proposition that individuals can make a difference. This proposition has never been universally accepted." The premise of this book is that individual school leaders who are concerned about education and committed to change, *can* and *do* make a difference in the education of America's youth.

"Them that's going, get in the goddamn wagon. Them that ain't, get out of the goddamn way."

—from "The Bear"
by William Faulkner

ACKNOWLEDGMENTS

Challenges for School Leaders is a publication of the American Association of School Administrators, the professional organization for more than 18,000 educational leaders across the United States, Canada, and other parts of the world. Without the enthusiastic support of AASA members, staff, and many others who contributed their experiences and opinions through surveys and interviews, this publication would not have been possible. AASA is particularly indebted to the association's Executive Committee and executive staff for assisting with the development of the contents of this publication. And AASA is grateful to the numerous education and reform experts and groups whose research and writings formed the bases of this work.

Kristen Amundson, a leading education writer in the Washington, D.C., area, served as author of this book. AASA Associate Executive Director Gary Marx initiated the project as a means of "making sense" of the myriad of reform reports and books on leadership and management. AASA Communications Projects Manager Luann Fulbright served as editor and production manager.

Headquarters for the American Association of School Administrators is located at 1801 North Moore Street, Arlington, Virginia 22209-9988; 703/528-0700.